T5-BPY-353

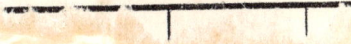
DATE DUE

CLAREMONT READING CONFERENCE

Sponsored by The Claremont Graduate School

FIFTY-FIRST YEARBOOK

Edited By
MALCOLM P. DOUGLASS

Special 1987 Conference theme:
**WRITING AND READING IN A
CULTURALLY DIVERSE SOCIETY**

Continuing Conference theme:
**READING, THE PROCESS OF CREATING
MEANING FOR SENSED STIMULI**

372.4
c541c
1987   cup

Price $20.00

Back issues of the Claremont Reading Conference are available from two sources. Volumes still in print may be ordered from the following address: Claremont Reading Conference Yearbook, Harper 200, Claremont Graduate School, Claremont, California 91711-6160. Write for information concerning books in print and special price list. All past Yearbooks are available through University Microfilms, 300 Zeeb Road, Ann Arbor, Michigan 48103.

ISBN #0-941742-05-9

Published by The Claremont Reading Conference
Center for Developmental Studies
Claremont Graduate School, Claremont, California 91711-6160

ii

Table of Contents

Introduction
to the 51st Yearbook

With this volume we are once again pleased to offer
the readership of these conference series reports a new
set of essays generated out of the annual Claremont
Reading Conference. Like the first of these meetings,
which was held in the summer of 1932, the 1987
Conference emphasized the naturalness of reading
behavior. But unlike the first, it was held in a time when
teaching reading as a process rather than a subject in
the school curriculum appears to be a much more widely
appreciated reality. Today, after years of insistence on
reaching the goal of universal literacy through teaching
which seeks to invoke reading behavior through formal
instruction, the idea that one learns to read primarily
through the practice of reading, and concurrently,
writing through the practice of writing, is gaining
acceptance. In these essays, the reader will find a
variety of ideas which underpin and expand upon the
basic premise of this conference series, that reading and
writing are *evoked* rather than *invoked* behaviors.

The reader will also find the special conference theme
for 1987, *Writing and Reading in a Culturally Diverse
Society,* emphasized in a number of articles appearing
in the present volume. Cultural diversity implies the
necessity of coexistence among differing values and
ways of life. It is essential that our schools respect those
differences while at the same time making possible the
achievement of full literacy for every child. Within these
essays the reader will find expressed ideas about the
nature and subtlety of that diversity which provides
both opportunity and problem for today's educationist.

Malcolm P. Douglass, *Director*
Claremont Reading Conference

Encouraging Free Reading

Stephen D. Krashen

There is widespread agreement that free, voluntary reading is beneficial. Studies have confirmed that students who do more free reading show superior levels of competence in reading, in vocabulary, writing style, and grammatical development. (1) There is good reason, in fact, to suspect that free reading is more than helpful — it may be the only way we develop competence in reading and in the conventions of writing. Independently derived theories of reading agree that "we learn to read by reading," (2) and my own work in language acquisition has led me to the hypothesis that we acquire language in only one way — by understanding messages or by receiving "comprehensible input" in a low anxiety environment. (3) This is precisely what free, voluntary reading is — comprehensible input in a low anxiety environment.

The consequences of this position are very serious. It means that the development of so-called "skills'" are a by-product of free reading. It means that drills and exercises, or "skill-building" programs, are only a test, a test that children who grow up in print-rich environments pass and that less fortunate children fail. It means that one of our major goals in language education should be to encourage free reading, to make sure it happens. Unfortunately, there has been little effort in this direction. Our major efforts, instead, have been directed at testing language "skills." The argument seems to be that more testing, "higher standards," and a tougher posture will somehow force an effort that will result in increased levels of literacy — children and teachers just need to try harder and change their lazy ways.

In my view, increased and more aggressive testing
has just the opposite effect — it hurts the development
of literacy. To see how this is so, let us assume that our
goal is to increase children's vocabulary. The popular
solution would be additional vocabulary testing (can
you imagine a new requirement — students need to
demonstrate that they know x number of words upon
high school graduation!). More vocabulary testing will
of course mean more direct teaching of vocabulary,
more vocabulary drills, exercises, and flash cards. But
drills and exercises are a very inefficient means of
building vocabulary. Nagy, Herman, and Anderson (4)
calculated that free reading is about 10 times as
effective as drills and exercises for acquiring
vocabulary; time devoted to direct vocabulary teaching
would be far more profitably spent reading, a much
more pleasant activity with many additional benefits.
Increased testing, then, all too often leads to increased
direct teaching and less reading and less progress in
language development.

Let us turn to what can be done to encourage reading.
I will begin with what is certainly the most obvious
strategy, but one that may be the most neglected: we
must make sure the books are there.

Access

Research supports the commonsense view that
children read more when there are more books around.
Morrow (5) reported modest but consistent correlations
between different measures of access to reading
material and the frequency with which children used
books during their free time at school: Children showed
more interest in books when the library corner was more
accessible, when books were within the child's reach,
when more new books were placed in the library corner,
and when teachers allowed the children to take books
home from the classroom library.

Morrow and Weinstein (6) reported that installing a
well-designed library corner in kindergarten classes
that previously did not have them resulted in
significantly increased "literature use" by children
during free play time, that is, more looking at books,

listening to stories, enacting a story that had been read to the class, or using literature props (roll movies, felt-board stories).

Morrow (7) also reported that children showing high interest in books had more books in their homes, universally had books in their room (compared to only 16.9 percent of children showing low interest in books), and were taken to the library far more frequently.

Neuman (8) reported similar findings among third graders. More leisure reading was correlated with greater amount of reading material available in the home, especially magazines and newspapers. Also consistent is Heyns (9) who found that children who lived closer to libraries read more.

A clever confirmation of the importance of access to books was provided by Powell, (10) who compared two elementary schools (grades 4, 5, and 6), one that emphasized classroom book collections and one that depended on a nearby public library. Both schools "encouraged wide recreatory reading" (p. 395) and had sustained silent reading programs. Students in the school that relied more on classroom libraries reported much more free reading, averaging 16 books per student during the first eight weeks of the school year, compared to 7.2 books per student in the other school. Powell attributes this difference to the fact that when classroom libraries are emphasized, "the students are surrounded by books" (p. 395) and concluded that "the more immediate the access to library material, the greater the amount of student recreatory reading" (p. 396).

A reasonable interpretation of these data is that access to books is necessary, but is not sufficient, for the development of literacy. Certainly, without reading material, little progress will be made. I suspect that the absence of books and other reading is one of the most serious problems we face in language education.

Comfort and quiet

Morrow's data (7) also suggest that the physical characteristics of the reading environment are important: pre-school and kindergarten children use the library corner more when it has pillows, easy chairs, and carpets, and when it is partitioned off, and when it is quiet. Children also show more interest in books when they are given class time to look at books.

Access to books in a comfortable and quiet place occurs, of course, in the library. Libraries are crucially important. There is good evidence that children get most of their books from some kind of library. In Table One, I combine data from three different studies (11) in which elementary school children were asked where they got their books for free reading. There is some variation in the data: in Lamme's study, for example, the school library was most popular, while in Ingram's outer city sample, the classroom library was used more. There is good agreement in all studies, however, that children get most of their reading from some kind of library. (Undoubtedly, ease of use, accessibility, and selection determine whether classroom, school, or public libraries are used more.)

TABLE ONE

Percentage of Books Children Obtain from Libraries (Public, School, or Classroom) for Pleasure Reading

age	9	10	11	12
study				
Lamme (1976)	88.7	83.7	81.4	
Ingham (1978)(1)		99.6	97.2	89.0
Ingham (1978)(2)		88.2	71.5	83.5
Swanton (1984)			70.2	

(1): outer city school   (2): inner city school

I suspect that many children do not have a quiet, comfortable place to read. There is often little peace and quiet at home, and public libraries may be too far away for smaller children. The solution, of course, is a well-stocked school library, a library that is open before school, during recess, during lunch, and, most important, after school (not 10 minutes but two hours) and over the summer vacation.

If free reading is as important as I suspect it is, additional school and classroom library resources are not a luxury — they are a necessity. The collections of most school libraries probably need to be doubled or tripled and library access vastly improved. (For additional suggestions on increasing access to books, see Veatch (12), pp. 592-607.)

Models

As Frank Smith (2) and McCracken and McCracken (13) have stated, reading needs to be demonstrated. Many children do not see people reading for pleasure. The research data are consistent with these suggestions. Morrow (5) found that more use of books was significantly correlated with teachers' participation in sustained silent reading — when the teachers read more, the students showed more interest in books. Similarly, both Morrow (7) and Neuman (8) report that parents of children who had high interest in books read more. While these data could be interpreted as showing that teachers and parents who model reading also do other things that encourage reading, it suggests that having a model is important. If this is true, it means that teachers need to follow McCracken and McCracken's advice (13) and actually read for pleasure during sustained silent reading time. This may be difficult, given the endless paperwork teachers have to deal with, but the sacrifice may be worth it!

Literature

Morrow (5) provides evidence that reading to children, discussing stories with them, and showing how fiction relates to other subjects are associated with interest in books. Similarly, Lomax (14) found that nursery school children who were particularly interested in books and stories heard more stories from their parents than children who were less interested in books and stories. According to Neuman's data (8), the amount of reading out loud to children when they are young correlates with their leisure reading habits when they are 10 years old — the effect of reading to children is apparently long-lasting.

Three experimental studies provide strong confirmation of the hypothesis that "literature activities" can increase student free reading. In Morrow and Weinstein (6), literature activities such as daily reading of stories, discussion of stories, and encouraging use of the library center were increased in kindergarten classrooms. Students in these experimental classes engaged in significantly more "literature use" (defined earlier) during free time than did students in comparison classes that engaged in no extra literature activities.

Morrow and Weinstein (15) reported similar results with second graders — more literature activities done by the teacher resulted in greater voluntary use of the library center — and the most popular activity at the library center was reading. Increasing literature use in the classroom did not result in more voluntary reading at home, however, a finding which Morrow and Weinstein suggest may be due to the fact that students' lives outside of school were already filled with other activities.

Pitts (16) reported that literature activities can stimulate reading in older readers; "basic skills" university students ("intelligent but underprepared students of all ages entering college for the first time," p. 37) were read to one hour per week for 13 weeks. Selections included works by Mark Twain, J.D. Salinger, Poe, and Thurber, and the reading was discussed afterwards. Pitts reported that the class that was read to checked out more books, and better books, from the reading lab than did students in the other basic skills classes. In addition, Pitts noted, "We know the books were read, not just carried around, because staff members were sought out daily by the students so they could discuss confusing sections and terminology and to share reactions" (p. 41).

I will conclude this survey with a brief report of another means of encouraging reading, one that involves exposing children to a kind of reading that school typically ignores: so-called "light reading."

Light reading

The data we have suggest that at worst, light reading causes no harm. It may, in fact, do some real good. There is evidence that light reading serves as a conduit to more "serious" reading, and sometimes is not as "light" as we think it is. I will focus here on what is probably the best-studied kind of light reading in the United States: comic books (for a fuller report, see Krashen). (17)

According to comic book historians, the "Golden Age" of comic books began in the late 1930s. The public had never been enthusiastic about comics (see, e.g., Zorbaugh, (18)), but it was Wertham's vicious attack (19) that was the major factor that sent comics into a decline. Wertham claimed that comics were a cause of reading disability (since readers only needed to look at the pictures), and comics provided a model for criminal and other forms of anti-social behavior. Research has not confirmed these accusations. Studies show only a weak or no relationship between comic book reading and problem behavior, (20) and there is no evidence that comic book readers do any worse in school. (21) In addition, comic book reading does not seem to take the place of other pleasure reading. Some studies show that comic book readers read as much as non-comic-book readers, while one study of seventh graders reported that comic readers actually read more. (22)

The complexity of comic book texts is variable. Some are quite challenging, reaching the sixth-grade level, while others are at the second-grade level. Deborah Krashen has pointed out to me that the still-popular *Archie* comics may be the best "high-interest-low-vocabulary" reading around. According to Wright, (23) *Archie* is written at about the second-grade level, but Archie and his friends Betty, Veronica, Jughead, and Reggie are high school students (after 46 years!).

There is good evidence that comics can encourage reading. The literature in this area includes Dorrell and Carroll's report (24) of a junior high school that stocked comics in the library but did not allow them to circulate: overall library traffic nearly doubled and circulation on non-comic-book library material increased about 30 percent!

Comics are doing much better these days. One reason for their renaissance is their improved quality. The "Silver Age" of comic books began in 1961, with the publication of Marvel Comics' *Fantastic Four,* followed in 1962 by what may have been the most important event in comic book history in the United States: the first appearance of Spider-Man. Under Stan Lee's leadership, Marvel developed the first superheroes with problems. Spider-Man, for example, has problems that the Superman and Batman of the 1940s and 1950s never imagined — money problems, women problems, and a lack of direction and self-esteem. Other Marvel characters are equally fascinating: the *X-Men,* mutants with special powers who are misunderstood and mistrusted by the public; *Squadron Supreme,* a "limited series" that dealt with a group of superheroes who try to prevent crime and other social problems by setting up a benevolent dictatorship. In doing this, they suppress individual rights, and the inevitable revolution occurs, with the former heroes becoming the villains, and former villains becoming the champions of the people!

Of course, not all comics are of high quality, but there is good evidence that at least this form of light reading has real benefits. The same may be true of other kinds of light reading. (25)

Conclusions

I am not claiming that free reading is a cure-all, only that it is essential. And I am not claiming that students should do only free reading — a personal reading program is only part of language arts. (1) There are also some serious problems with the solutions proposed here:

1. Library budgets are often limited.
2. No textbook publisher gets rich when students read trade books.
3. Free reading seems to be too easy. It may be hard for some people to believe that such a pleasant activity is so beneficial.

4. Results may not be immediate. If a teacher succeeds in encouraging a child to read, next year's teacher will probably see the benefits and get the credit!

Somehow we have to solve these problems. We have no choice.

REFERENCES

1 Krashen, Stephen. *Inquiries and Insights: Essays on Language Teaching, Bilingual Education, and Literacy* (Alemany Press, 1985).

2 Smith, Frank. *Understanding Reading* (Hold Rinehart Winston, 1982).

  Goodman, Kenneth. *Language and Literacy* (Routledge and Kegan Paul, 1982).

3 Krashen, Stephen. *The Input Hypothesis: Issues and Implications* (Longman, 1985).

4 Nagy, William; Herman, Patricia; and Anderson, Richard. "Learning words from context" *Reading Research Quarterly,* 1985, *20*: 233-253.

5 Morrow, Leslie. "Relationships between literature programs, library corner designs, and children's use of literature" *Journal of Educational Research,* 1982, *75*: 339-344.

6 Morrow, Leslie, and Weinstein, Carol. "Increasing children's use of literature through program and physical changes" *The Elementary School Journal,* 1982, *83*: 131-137.

7 Morrow, Leslie. "Home and school correlates of early interest in literature" *Journal of Educational Research,* 1983, *76*: 221-230.

8 Neuman, Susan. "The home environment and fifth-grade students' leisure reading" *The Elementary School Journal,* 1986, *86*: 335-343.

9 Heyns, Barbara. *Summer Learning and the Effects of Schooling* (Academic Press, 1978).

10 Powell, William. "Classroom libraries: their frequency of use" *Elementary English,* 1966, *43*: 395-397.

11 Lamme, Linda. "Are reading habits and abilities related?" *The Reading Teacher,* 1976, *30*: 21-27.

  Ingham, Jennie. *Books and Reading Development: The Bradford Book Flood Experiment* (Heinemann Educational Books Ltd., 1981).

  Swanton, Susan. "Minds alive: what and why gifted students read for pleasure" *School Library Journal,* 1984, *30*: 99-102.

12 Veatch, Jeannette. *Reading in the Elementary School.* Second Edition. (Wiley, 1978).

13 McCracken, Robert, and McCracken, Marlene. "Modeling is the key to sustained silent reading" *The Reading Teacher,* 1978, *31*: 406-408.

14 Lomax, Carol. "Interest in books and stories at nursery school" *Educational Research,* 1976, *19:* 100-112.

15 Morrow, Leslie, and Weinstein, Carol. "Encouraging voluntary reading: The impact of a literature program on children's use of library centers" *Reading Research Quarterly,* 1986, *21:* 330-346.

16 Pitts, Sandra Kelton. "Read aloud to adult learners? Of course!" *Reading Psychology: An International Quarterly,* 1986, 7: 35-42.

17 Krashen, Stephen. *Comic Book Reading and Language Development* (Abel Press, 1987).

18 Zorbaugh, Harvey. "What adults think of comics as reading for children" *The Journal of Educational Sociology,* 1949, *23,* 225-235.

19 Wertham, Fredric. *Seduction of the Innocent.* (Rinehart and Company, 1955).

20 Witty, Paul. "Reading the comics — comparative study" *Journal of Experimental Education,* 1941, *10:* 105-109.

Blakely, W. Paul. ' A study of seventh grade children's reading of comic books as related to certain other variables" *Journal of Genetic Psychology, 1958, 93:* 291-301.

Hoult, Thomas. "Comic books and juvenile delinquency" *Sociology and Social Research,* 1949, *33:* 279-284.

21 Witty, Paul. "Reading the comics — a comparative study."

Blakely, W. Paul. "A study of seventh grade children's reading of comic books, as related to certain other variables."

Heisler, Florence. "A comparison of comic book and non-comic-book readers of the elementary school" *Journal of Educational Research,* 1947, *40:* 458-464.

22 Blakely, W. Paul. "A study of seventh grade children's reading of comic books, as related to certain other variables."

23 Wright, Gary. "The comic book — a forgotten medium in the classroom" *The Reading Teacher,* 1979, *33:* 158-161.

24 Dorrell, Larry, and Carroll, Ed. "Spider-Man at the Library" *School Library Journal,* 1981, *27:* 17-19.

25 Parrish, Berta, and Atwood, Karen. "Enticing readers: the teen romance craze" *The California Reader,* 1985, *18:* 22-27.

A Conceptual Framework for Integrated Literacy Teaching

Stephen B. Kucer

The manner in which reading and writing are taught has become fairly standardized in most American schools. Typically, mornings are spent instructing children in those skills which are thought to be crucial to the development of literacy. In an attempt to make this learning easy for the children, reading and writing are: 1) taught as unrelated processes, 2) divided into discrete subskills stripped of meaning, 3) presented to the children in a piecemeal fashion, and 4) isolated from the content fields of literature, science, and the social sciences. While the ultimate goal is to assist students in making meaning through and from print, this goal is set aside until the pre-requisite literacy skills have been explicitly taught and mastered.

Recent research in reading, writing, and learning would suggest that such an approach to the teaching of reading and writing needs to be re-evaluated. Rather than supporting student learning, segmented and isolated literacy curricula frequently produce students with segmented and isolated knowledge. For many of our students, the schooling experience results in little more than a tangle of skills and facts for which they can see no interrelationship or function. Similar to the king's men in "Humpty Dumpty," both the children and teachers must expend great amounts of time and energy if all of the curriculum pieces are to be put back together. A return to the so called basics will only increase the number of pieces to be taught and mastered and lead to more confusion for students and teachers.

There is a way, however, to avoid having to put Humpty Dumpty back together and that is by simply not taking him apart. In life, communication and learning are integrated, holistic processes. We read in order to discover new things or for pure enjoyment, not to master vocabulary or to practice our word attack skills. We write to record our thoughts or to communicate with others, not to test how well we can spell. It is through this process of reading and writing for meaning that we come to learn new vocabulary, new word attack skills, and new spellings. But even more importantly, it is through reading and writing that we come to learn more about the world in which we live. The real basics in life are not the skills and facts listed on a scope and sequence chart, but the ability to effectively use reading and writing to communicate and learn.

Many teachers and administrators have become disenchanted with current reading and writing instruction and are looking for ways to put the real basics back into the school literacy curriculum. Thematic units provide one practical and efficient way in which this can be accomplished (Busching & Schwartz, 1983; Cadenhead & Carmichael, 1979; Hardt, 1984; Moss, 1984). In thematic units, literacy is taught and learned through the study of topics or themes. The focus of each unit is not on teaching reading and writing as separate subjects, but on helping students to learn more about the topic through the use of literacy. All materials and activities are conceptually linked to the theme and, as illustrated in Figure 1, come not only from the basal reader, but also from the fields of literature, science, and the social sciences. Learning is enhanced in thematic teaching, because students repeatedly encounter a core set of interrelated meanings throughout the unit.

The purpose of this article is to develop a more integrated alternative to the teaching of reading and writing in the elementary school. Building upon current research in literacy and learning, I discuss eight guidelines for developing and implementing thematic units in the classroom. Because there are many different ways in which integration can be accomplished, these

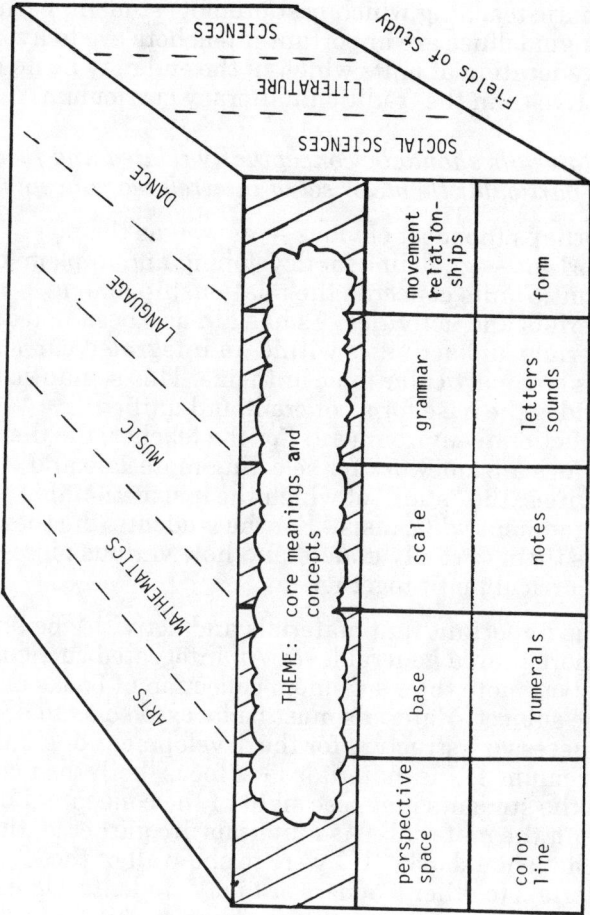

Figure 1: An integrated view of the curriculum. Note: Adapted from Harste, J., Woodward, V., and Burke, C. *Language stories and literacy lessons.* Portsmouth, N.H.: Heinemann, p. 207.

guidelines serve to highlight those characteristics of thematic teaching which best promote student learning. Such guidelines are important if teachers are to avoid the generation of units which in the end may be no more effective than the traditional literacy curriculum.

1. *Materials should be conceptually related and focus on a particular theme or set of interrelated concepts.*

Perhaps the most obvious — as well as the most important — guideline for developing and implementing thematic units concerns the relationship among materials and activities. As has already been noted, materials and activities within an integrated curriculum focus on a particular topic or theme. This semantic link provides the base for a coherent and unified instructional environment. For the teacher, the theme provides a framework for selecting materials and activities, the "stuff" of which the instructional environment will consist. For the students, the theme helps them to easily understand how various pieces of the curriculum fit together.

It is important that materials and activities be linked on more than a general level. An integrated curriculum involves more than a random collection of books on the same subject. Materials must be focused so as to provide the necessary structure for the development of a unified curriculum. If the materials lack focus, both the teacher and the students may lose sight of the conceptual link among the materials. As materials are gathered, the teacher should ask: "If I were to show all of these materials to other teachers or to my students, would they be able to guess the theme?"

In addition, the materials should offer the potential for being arranged in a meaningful instructional sequence. Since the teacher will use these materials to develop a series of activities, the materials need to build upon and extend each other. The teacher should ask: "What are the various ways and sequences in which I might present these materials to my students?"

It is important for the teacher to realize that theme selection and the gathering of materials are not separate processes. While the teacher will have an initial theme in mind when materials are collected, this theme will often be modified as materials are analyzed. As well, it is often difficult to know how well materials will link with one another until they have all been gathered. Therefore, it is usually best to simply begin collecting any and all materials which may be relevant to the theme. Once a number of materials have been gathered, the teacher can refine the theme if necessary and decide which materials provide the necessary focus as well as potential links to other materials.

Finally, materials should not be limited to textbooks currently being used in the classroom. The teacher should attempt to gather materials from a variety of resources — magazines, newspapers, encyclopedias, trade books — and include nonprint materials as well — maps, globes, cartoons, pictures, music. A good theme gives students opportunities to interact with the kinds of materials which are encountered in the world.

2. *Materials and activities should represent a variety of fields of study — sciences, literature, and the social sciences.*

As the teacher selects materials for the unit, he or she will want to include those from a variety of fields of study. A good thematic unit uses materials from the sciences and the social sciences as well as from literature. (See Figure 1.) Even when the theme has a particular subject matter focus, materials from other fields of study should be considered. For example, when teaching a unit on "Growing Plants and Seeds" to a third-grade class, I did not limit my materials to the sciences. I also used such literary texts as "Jack and the Beanstalk" and "The Great Big Enormous Turnip" and social science articles on the influence of vegetation on culture which came from National Geographic *World* magazine. Again, the focus is on integration, in this case the integration of various fields of study.

The incorporation of materials from various fields of study into the unit has a number of benefits for the students. First, it helps them to develop a fuller understanding of the theme. Because professionals in different fields view the world from unique perspectives, both what they have to say about a topic and how they say it will vary. The botanist's understanding of growing plants and seeds is different from the geographer's, and both differ from a writer of short stories. Given these unique perspectives, the thematic information which each piece of material presents will vary depending on the field from which it comes. As students interact with materials from different fields, they will develop a deeper understanding of the theme.

In addition, because each field of study views the same concept from various perspectives, the written materials in each field may also reflect the use of different organizational patterns. Science materials are often informational in nature while social science materials are frequently time-ordered. Literary materials may reflect narrative patterns as well as poetic and dramatic ones. These various types of organizational patterns make different kinds of demands on the reader or writer. If students are to learn to effectively use these patterns, they must be encountered in the thematic unit. As students read and write using these various organizational patterns, not only will their knowledge of the topic increase, but their reading and writing will also improve.

3. *Students should be given opportunities to generate meanings using a variety of communication systems — language, art, music, dance, and mathematics.*

In thematic teaching the concept of literacy is expanded to include all of the communication systems. As illustrated in Figure 1, students use not only language to communicate and learn, but also art, music, dance, and mathematics. Just as each field of study has its own unique way of looking at a particular topic, each communication system has its own unique way of expressing ideas. When planning a thematic unit, the teacher should seek ways to have students express what they have learned through various systems. As students cross the communication systems, they will learn about how the systems operate and at the same time discover new insights into the meanings which they are trying to

express. In a thematic unit, there are a variety of
perspectives from which the students will come to
understand the topic and multiple ways in which they
will learn to express these understandings (Eisner, 1982;
Suhor, 1984).

An example of what is meant by expressing meaning
through a variety of communication systems I think
will help clarify this guideline. When teaching the unit
on "Growing Plants and Seeds," I read Tolstoy's "Great
Big Enormous Turnip" to the children. At a key point in
the story I stopped reading and had the children
brainstorm the possible ways in which the main
character might solve his problem. After listing all the
possible solutions on the board, each child was given a
booklet of blank paper and asked to complete the story
through pictures. When the illustrations were complete,
the children shared their picture books and we
compared endings. We then read Tolstoy's version and
discussed how his ending and use of pictures was
similar/dissimilar to the students'. In the days
following this activity the children also wrote poems
and songs about the story, grew and measured the
growth of turnip seeds, illustrated through movement
and music key parts of the story, and compared and
contrasted other plant stories we had read, such as
"Jack and the Beanstalk," with "The Great Big
Enormous Turnip." In these activities, the children
created meaning through language, mathematics, art,
music, and dance. In the process of doing so, not only
did the children come to more fully understand the
story, but they also learned about numerals and
measurement, color, line, and space, scales and notes,
grammar, letters, and sounds, and form, movement, and
relationships. (See Figure 1.)

4. *Materials and activities should encourage the
students to build and integrate meanings from a variety
of sources and experiences.*

Comprehension involves a process of integration
(Anderson, Spiro, & Montague, 1977; Smith, 1975; Spiro,
Bruce, & Brewer, 1980). The learner must link new
meanings and ideas to what is already known about the
topic. In a sense, this involves a "marriage" between old
and new information. The more that is known about the

topic, the better the marriage. Because materials and activities in a thematic unit are conceptually related, students have the opportunity to build the background knowledge which is necessary for comprehension to occur.

However, not only must the necessary background knowledge be available, but students must be willing to use it. Students must experience activities which encourage them to apply what they already know. Therefore, the teacher should consider three questions as activities for the theme are developed: 1) What background knowledge has the theme already provided which the students can draw upon when engaged in this activity?, 2) How does the activity make the students use this knowledge?, and 3) What new knowledge will the students learn from this experience which can be used as a base for future activities? In asking these questions the teacher will come to view each activity not as a separate or isolated lesson, but as an event with a past and a future.

Requiring students to use previous experiences when engaged in current activities not only promotes learning in the present, but also enhances understanding of the past. Returning to past experiences helps the students to rethink what was learned and to develop a clearer understanding of the past in light of the present. This is similar to what happens when we reread a favorite book or rewrite a paper for a class. When rereading or rewriting we are not the same person. We are different, if only due to having done the initial reading or writing, and know what to expect when we return to the book or paper. Such a change in our background knowledge allows us to stand back from the text and see things that were not seen the first time. Comprehension, therefore, becomes an ongoing event. It is not finished when the lesson is complete, but continues to grow as students use what they have learned in new settings. This "recycling" of meaning throughout the theme is the counterpart to the practice, master, and reinforcement which usually happens in the classroom. In thematic units, rather than simply repeating activities over and over the students use meanings from previous experiences when engaged in new activities.

Finally, not only does a wealth of background knowledge lead to better learning, but it also leads to better reading and writing. Research has clearly shown that when students have the necessary background knowledge, they read and write better (Crafton, 1981; Langer, 1984; Pearson & Tierney, 1984; Rousch, 1976). Thematic units take advantage of this relationship by helping students build up background knowledge which can be used when interacting with print.

5. *The focus of the curriculum should be on learning and using key reading and writing processes.*

As activities are developed for the theme, the teacher will want to consider what reading and writing processes need to be included in the unit. Research in reading and writing has identified a number of critical processes which must be learned if literacy growth is to take place (Allen & Watson, 1976; Birnbaum, 1982; Goodman & Burke, 1980; Graves, 1983; Kucer, 1985; Smith, 1982a, 1982b; Tierney & Pearson, 1983). As activities for the unit are considered, the teacher should ask: "What reading or writing processes will my students need to use in order to be successful with this activity?" In asking this question, the teacher will be able to keep in mind the needs of the students as activities are developed.

During the last decade, a number of proponents of whole language have advocated the use of such processes as the base for teaching reading and writing (Cochrane, Cochrane, Scalena, & Buchanan, 1984; Goodman & Burke, 1980; Graves, 1983; Newman, 1986). These processes are never taught in isolation from the other processes, but are used to read or write whole texts. The focus of each lesson is on the creation of meaning and knowledge and not on the process itself. Thematic units extend whole language and the use of these processes by embedding them in a more unified curriculum.

Once again, an example of what a whole language lesson might look like in a thematic unit will help make this guideline clear. As I developed activities for the "Growing Plants and Seeds" unit, I was concerned that too many of the students had difficulty comprehending what they had read in an organized manner. Similarly, their writing was often unstructured. I therefore developed a reading and writing activity which focused on the organization of meaning. I took the book, "Jack and the Beanstalk," divided it into separate pages, and xeroxed several copies of each page. The students were then put into groups of four and given a copy of the segmented story in random order. The groups were told that their job was to find a meaningful order in which to put the pages. After all groups had finished, we compared and discussed the various sequences with a focus on whether the texts, as structured, made sense.

In writing, I had the students take a copy of a story they had written and cut it up by paragraphs. After shuffling, students exchanged paragraphs with a partner. Each partner then became a "reader" and arranged the paragraphs in a meaningful order. Once the partner had constructed a meaningful sequence, he or she explained the order to the author and gave reasons for the order. The author then took back his or her own paragraphs, put them in the original order, and also explained the reasons. Finally, the partners discussed ways in which each story could be organized in a more meaningful way and revisions were made. As is evident, while the focus was on integrating meaning, the students still needed to use a number of other processes to successfully complete these lessons. In addition, the students read and wrote whole texts which were related to the theme.

6. *Activities should be social as well as individual in nature. Students should be given opportunities to construct meaning in collaborative situations.*

Learning in general, and literacy learning in particular, involves interaction and communication with others (Dewey, 1973; Vygotsky, 1978). There would be little need for a child to develop language in a nonsocial environment. Therefore, thematically-based classrooms need to provide a rich social environment which gives students opportunities to work together, to exchange ideas, and to engage in the mutual construction of meaning.

While individual and whole class activities are part of a thematically-based curriculum, small group work provides one of the best ways in which social interaction can be encouraged in the classroom. In addition, working with others allows the child to accomplish tasks which could not be done independently. With the support of others, the child becomes "a head taller than himself" (Vygotsky, 1978, p. 102).

The grouping of students should go beyond the use of reading groups in which most students stay for the entire year. Rather, groups should be formed and reformed as the needs and interests of the students arise. Rhodes (1983) has suggested a number of ways in which grouping can be done in the classroom.

Grouping can be based on particular interests which various members of a class might have. For example, in the unit on "Growing Plants and Seeds," students were broken into groups to investigate the parts of a seed, the differences between fruits and vegetables, the role which sunlight, water, fertilizer, and temperature play in growing seeds, and the various items in society which are produced from plants and seeds.

Another way in which interest groups can be formed is to have Books of the Month Club. The teacher and students select a number of books of interest which are related to the theme under study. Each student is then asked to join a group based on the book being read. These groups can be formed and reformed as books are finished and new interests arise.

Groups can also be based on the reading and writing needs of the students; the teacher can develop lessons for certain processes for various groups of students. This same type of grouping can be done when students are experiencing difficulty understanding or using key concepts or thinking processes.

Friendship groups can be used as well. This type of grouping allows students to work with their friends which is sure to encourage social interaction but within a structured environment. When using this type of group, the teacher will want to take care that the instructional activity is well-defined so that the interaction among the friends is directed toward the goal of the lesson.

Finally, as was done in the reading activity discussed under guideline five, students can be put into groups to do the same activity and then be brought together as a class to share and discuss their results. This type of grouping is especially helpful when the teacher is trying to help students understand a concept from a number of different perspectives.

7. *The unit should build upon and extend the experiences and interests of the students; there should be a continuity of experience.*

The selection of the theme and its activities are not solely determined by the teacher; students also have input. Thematic teaching not only involves the integration of reading and writing with the content areas, but also the integration of the child's home and community experiences with classroom experiences. Dewey (1973) termed this linking of the home and school the continuity of experience. He argued that while the school was responsible for extending the experiences of the child, the experiences which the child brought to the school were to serve as the foundation for this extension. Therefore, as the teacher considers possible themes and activities, he or she will want to find ways to bring the world into the classroom.

In most cases, the selection of themes based on student interest can be done informally. Teachers are readily aware when a new interest sweeps the classroom. During free time, children can be found discussing current movies, television shows, games, or family trips. These interests are frequently reflected in the types of books that are selected from the library, in the topics which are written about, or in the games played during recess. The teacher need not give a formal interest inventory to discover these interests; simply observing and listening to the children can provide this information. When themes and activities are built on these "at home" experiences, students can more readily build a bridge between the school and the home.

Themes of interest can also emerge from previously taught units. Rather than changing abruptly from one topic to another, the teacher may wish to take an idea generated during another unit and develop a new unit. This not only provides a linkage among the units, but also takes into account student interests. In the unit on "Growing Plants and Seeds," the children became interested in how clothing was made. This interest served as the base for a later unit.

Using students' interests as the foundation for unit development does not mean that the teacher must construct entirely new themes each year. There are certainly topics which are of inherent interest to almost all elementary children, such as themes on growing up, conflict, photography, or animals. These themes can be taught year after year, with the teacher simply modifying each unit based on the students being taught. At the same time, the teacher can develop new units in response to the unique interests of the students.

Finally, the interests of the teacher should be considered. Most teachers have hobbies or personal interests which the children will find appealing. Some of the most popular themes in a class are those in which the teacher has personal interest. In these situations, the teacher's enthusiasm for the topic becomes infectious and the students carry the interest home. Therefore, as themes and activities are selected, the teacher should ask: "What are the interests of the students and myself?"

Just this sort of interaction between home and school occurred in the unit on "Growing Plants and Seeds." Not only did we take walks to discover and collect plants and seeds in the children's neighborhood, but the children also brought seeds from home to grow in the classroom. Because many of the seeds brought from home reflected the cultural eating habits of the students, this naturally led to class discussion on diet and nutrition. Also, the fact that many of the students were recent immigrants from Central and South America provided us with the opportunity to compare the local vegetation in Southern California with their countries of birth. Finally, many of the students brought seeds home and started windowbox gardens of their own. It is just this type of interaction between school and home which the teacher will want to encourage.

8. *The unit should provide students with opportunities for independent learning, problem-solving, and risk-taking.*

A major goal of schooling is to produce individuals who can continue to learn without the teacher. Basic to independent learning is the willingness to take risks: to try something new, to evaluate one's work, and to then be willing to try again. Without the making of mistakes, there is no learning. If independence is to be fostered in the classroom, students must be given opportunities to make mistakes and learn from them. This requires an environment in which the making of mistakes is not penalized, but rather understood for what they are: attempts on the part of the child to stretch beyond what he or she is currently capable of doing.

Teachers can encourage this stretching in a number of ways. First, when evaluating student work, the teacher should focus on what the student can or is attempting to do, rather than on what the student doesn't know or can't do. An appreciation for the attempts of the student encourages subsequent attempts and also helps the teacher understand the thinking behind the child's behavior.

Secondly, the teacher can involve students in experiences which require problem-solving and discovery-learning. Telling students how to do something is usually not as effective as allowing students to figure it out for themselves. As was discussed under guideline six, this does not necessarily require that students work alone. Social interaction and teamwork within a structured environment allow students to share their thoughts and to get immediate feedback.

Finally, independent learning can be encouraged by developing activities which are open-ended. There are usually a number of ways in which problems can be solved. Allowing students to generate and share various solutions gives students new insights into the problem.

In the "Growing Plants and Seeds" unit, students were provided such opportunities when they worked in groups to organize the segmented story of "Jack and the Beanstalk" and when I had them dissect a seed in order to discover its parts.

Summary

While the previous eight guidelines provide the teacher with a framework to use as thematic units are developed, they are not intended to be exclusive. The teacher will want to add to these guidelines as he or she becomes more comfortable with the use of thematic units in the classroom. Also, the guidelines are only that, guidelines, and should be modified or ignored when necessary. This is especially true for the teacher just beginning to use themes in the classroom. In these situations, it is usually best if the teacher selects just some of the guidelines. Once the teacher has more experience with this type of teaching, more of the guidelines can be incorporated into the units, as well as additional guidelines which the teacher finds to be helpful.

REFERENCES

Allen, D. & Watson D., (Eds.). *Findings of research in miscue analysis: Classroom implications.* Urbana, Ill.: National Council of Teachers of English.

Anderson, R., Spiro, R., & Montague, W. (Eds.). (1977). *Schooling and the acquisition of knowledge.* Hillsdale, N.J.: Erlbaum.

Birnbaum, J. (1982). The reading and composing behaviors of selected fourth- and seventh-grade students. *Research in the Teaching of English, 16,* 241-260.

Busching, B. & Schwartz, J. (Eds.). (1983). *Integrating the language arts in the elementary school.* Urbana, Ill.: National Council of Teachers of English.

Cadenhead, K. & Carmichael, N. (1979). Emphasizing reading comprehension through the use of selected themes in children's literature. *Reading World, 19,* 63-71.

Cochrane, O., Cochrane, D., Scalena, S., & Buchanan, E. (1984). *Reading, Writing and Caring.* New York, N.Y.: Richard C. Owens.

Crafton, L. (1981). *The reading process as a transactional experience.* Unpublished doctoral dissertation, Indiana University.

Dewey, J. (1973). *Experience and education.* New York, N.Y.: Collier Books.

Eisner, E. (1982). *Cognition and Curriculum.* New York, N.Y.: Longman.

Goodman, Y. & Burke, C. (1980). *Reading strategies: Focus on comprehension.* New York, N.Y.: Holt, Rinehart & Winston.

Graves, D. (1983). *Writing: Teachers and children at work.* Exeter, N.H.: Heinemann.

Hardt, U. (Ed.). (1984). *Teaching reading with the other language arts.* Newark, Del.: International Reading Association.

Kucer, S. (1985). The making of meaning: Reading and writing as parallel processes. *Written Communication, 2,* 317-336.

Langer, J. (1984). The effects of available information on responses to school writing tasks. *Research in the Teaching of English, 18,* 27-44.

Moss, J. (1984). *Focus units in literature: A handbook for elementary school teachers.* Urbana, Ill.: National Council of Teachers of English.

Newman, J. (Ed.). (1986). *Whole language: Theory in use.* Portsmouth, N.H.: Heinemann.

Pearson, D. & Tierney, R. (1984). Learning to read like a writer. In A. Purves & O. Niles (Eds.), *Becoming readers in a complex society.* Eighty-third Yearbook of the National Society for the Study of Education. Chicago, Ill.: National Society for the Study of Education.

Rhodes, L. (1983). Organizing the elementary classroom for effective language learning. In U. Hardt (Ed.), *Teaching reading with the other language arts.* Newark, Del.: International Reading Association.

Rousch, P. (1976). Testing. In D. Allen & D. Watson (Eds.), *Findings of research in miscue analysis: Classroom implications.* Urbana, Ill.: National Council of Teachers of English.

Smith, F. (1975). *Comprehension and learning.* New York, N.Y.: Holt, Rinehart & Winston.

Smith, F. (1982a). *Understanding reading.* N.Y.: Holt, Rinehart & Winston.

Smith, F. (1982b). *Writing and the writer.* N.Y.: Holt, Rinehart & Winston.

Spiro, R., Bruce, B., & Brewer, W. (Eds.). (1980). *Theoretical issues in reading comprehension.* Hillsdale, N.J.: Erlbaum.

Suhor, C. (1984). *Towards a semiotics-based curriculum. Curriculum Studies, 16,* 247-257.

Tierney, R. & Pearson, P.D. (1983). Toward a composing model of reading. *Language Arts, 60,* 568-580.

Vygotsky, L. (1978). *Mind in society.* M. Cole, V. John-Steiner, & E. Souberman (Eds. and trans.), Cambridge, Mass.: Harvard University Press.

Understanding the Motive To Achieve Among Mexican Americans

Raymond Buriel

I Euro-American conformity and the cultural integration hypothesis

Despite its claims to objectivity, social science research often reflects and legitimizes the prevailing ideologies of Euro-American society. Nowhere is this more apparent than in America's viewpoint regarding the assimilation of ethnic/cultural minorities. According to Gordon (1964), Euro-American conformity extolls the presumed superiority of the English language and Euro-American cultural patterns. A central assumption of this viewpoint is that success in this society is dependent upon a total rejection of inferior foreign cultures and a complete embracing of Euro-American culture.

The "damaging-culture" model is the social science analogue of society's Euro-American conformity ideology. This model is characteristic of studies which selectively focus on the problems of the Mexican-American population and which then use stereotypic descriptions of Mexican-American culture to explain the problems of this group. Thus, if Mexican-Americans do poorly in school, it is because their culture allegedly discourages achievement motivation (Demos, 1962); if they are economically disadvantged, it is because their culture encourages fatalism (Kuvlesky & Patella, 1971), and, if they are involved in gangs or other forms of delinquent activities, it is because of the anti-social and violent nature of their culture (Heller, 1966). On the other hand, in those rare instances where the social

27

science literature does report something favorable about
Mexican-Americans, the findings are either discounted
due to errors in methodology, or ascribed to the highly
acculturated nature of the Mexican-American subjects.
In no case is the favorable behavior associated with
Mexican-American culture. The results of the damaging-
culture studies have led social scientists to conclude that
Mexican-Americans need to assimilate in order to
ameliorate their problems and achieve upward mobility
in this society. Thus, operating under the guise of
objectivity, the results of damaging-culture studies
impart "scientific" legitimacy upon society's Euro-
American conformity ideology and strengthen its
position as a valid public policy to pursue toward
ethnic/cultural minorities. In the case of Mexican-
Americans, this means that successful adjustment to
American society is presumed to necessitate complete
disassociation from their ancestral culture.

Contrary to the assimilationist prescriptions of Euro-
American conformity ideology, this paper argues in
favor of the view that integration with immigrant
Mexican-American culture is conducive to success and
adjustment in this society. This paradoxical-sounding
argument is referred to as the "cultural integration
hypothesis" (Buriel, 1984). Essentially, the cultural
integration hypothesis holds that immigrant Mexican-
American culture is highly achievement oriented and
therefore compatible with the achievement demands of
United States society. It follows, therefore, that for
Mexican-Americans, assimilation is not a necessary
prerequisite for success and adjustment in society.

The cultural integration hypothesis is formulated on
the following points:

1. Mexican immigration to the United States is
   selective in nature and motivated by a desire for
   change, upward mobility, and achievement.
2. Immigrant Mexican-American culture arose
   primarily from the values and lifestyles of Mexican
   immigrants.
3. The achievement-oriented nature of immigrant
   Mexican-American culture is conducive to success
   and adjustment in United States society.

4. Due to intense pressures to assimilate, the core values of Mexican immigrants may be eroded over time and result in less traditional variations of Mexican-American culture.

5. Persons of Mexican descent may become "deculturated" if they lose contact with their ancestral culture and also fail to adopt Euro-American culture.

6. A state of deculturation greatly diminishes an individual's chances for conventionally defined success and adjustment in United States society.

The remainder of this paper will elaborate on each of these points by reviewing the empirical evidence in support of the cultural integration hypothesis. However, before proceeding, it is necessary to clarify the intended meaning of certain terms and concepts used in the paper.

A. Definition of terms and concepts

1. *Mexican-Americans* are persons of Mexican descent living in the United States. They acknowledge a Mexican, as opposed to Spanish, ancestry and are for the most part either immigrants or descendants of twentieth-century immigrants. They are a heterogeneous population that is stratified on a number of variables such as generational status, Spanish language usage and proficiency, and regionally related identities.

2. *Mexican-American Culture.* The diversity of the Mexican-American population precludes a description of a homogeneous Mexican-American culture that exerts a uniform level of influence on the lives of all its members. Instead, we can conceptualize it as consisting of different levels of affiliation with a core set of values and behaviors. In the center of the core are those values and behaviors which are prototypically Mexican-American in character. In the outer layers are values that represent steadily decreasing levels of affiliation to immigrant values.

3. *Immigrant Mexican-American Culture* is conceptualized as arising from the values and behaviors of Mexican immigrants to the United States. Although

Mexicanos and *Hispanos* were present in the Southwest prior to the Mexican-American War, today the overwhelming majority are descendants of twentieth-century immigrants. Consequently, immigrant Mexican-American culture is reflected in the values and lifestyles of the immigrants. And, since immigration is motivated by a desire for change, upward mobility, and achievement (Fromm & Maccoby, 1970), it is this set of achievement-oriented values which constitute immigrant Mexican-American culture, and which form the bedrock of Mexican-American culture in general. Other values that are central include a sense of familism, personalismo, hierarchical family roles, and affiliation with Mexican Catholic ideology (Ramirez & Castaneda, 1974). It should be noted that the influence of immigrant Mexican-American culture is probably greatest in the states of California and Texas since these two areas of the country have experienced, and continue to experience, the highest rates of Mexican immigration. Consequently, the ideas and conclusions expressed in this paper may only by relevant to the Mexican-American population living in these two states.

4. *Cultural Integration* refers to the degree to which an individual's behavior is influenced by immigrant Mexican-American culture. This paper does not conceptualize it as being the polar opposite of mainstream Euro-American culture. Consequently, an individual's level of cultural integration is not inevitably inversely related to his or her level of acculturation with Euro-American culture. In other words, one's level of cultural integration does not impose limits on the level of involvement with Euro-American culture.

5. *Acculturation* is the process of learning the social patterns and language of another cultural group. In the case of Mexican-Americans, it refers to their level of involvement and competence in Euro-American culture. It is therefore possible to be both highly accultured and culturally integrated; that is, bicultural. A bicultural person is one who is involved and competent in two cultural systems.

6. *Assimilation* is usually described as a unidirectional process involving rejection of one cultural system and absorption into another. For Mexican-Americans, assimilation represents a total abandonment of the ancestral culture and the complete adoption of Euro-American cultural patterns including values, religious beliefs, social practices, the English language, and an exclusive sense of "American" identity (as opposed to a Mexican-American, Chicano, or Hispanic identity). In effect, the assimilated person feels that he or she is no longer a member of an ethnic group but instead an amalgamated member of the Euro-American population and culture.

7. *Success and Adjustment.* Adaptation to United States society is measured in terms of socioeconomic success and psychological adjustment. The traditional socioeconomic indicators of occupational status, income, and education are used to define *success* in this paper. These indicators are relevant to a discussion of Mexican-American adaptation inasmuch as they represent the aspirations of Mexican immigrants. From Gamio's (1931) groundbreaking research on Mexican immigration in the 1920s to the more contemporary work of Cornelius and his associates (1982), the primary reasons cited for immigration include economic enhancement of the family and greater educational opportunities for children. It seems reasonable, therefore, to measure adaptation in terms of the goals that immigrants have established for themselves and their children. In addition, since conventionally defined forms of deviancy usually interfere with occupational and educational attainment, noninvolvement in deviant behavior represents an indirect measure of successful adaptation. *Adjustment* refers to the general psychological well being of people. At the personal level it involves the individual's feelings of self-worth and his or her state of mental health. In a broader context, though, it involves harmonious relationships within the family and with members of society.

8. *Deculturation,* according to Barry (1980), exists whenever individuals or groups are out of cultural and psychological contact with either their ancestral culture

or the larger society. In the case of Mexican-Americans, it describes a small minority of individuals who lack the necessary sociocultural skills to cope effectively with either the Mexican-American or Euro-American cultural systems. Deculturation arises initially from society's halfhearted efforts to assimilate Mexican-Americans. On the one hand, individuals are drawn away from immigrant Mexican-American culture on the pretext that it is unsuited for success and adjustment in this society. On the other, they are refused full participation in American society. As a result, they are left stranded in an anomic state where they feel betrayed by the larger society and at the same time, out of touch with the mainstream of their ancestral culture. Individuals do not voluntarily decide to become deculturated. Over time, however, the unique lifestyle associated with this state of affairs may become a source of pride and ethnic identity for some Mexican-Americans. When it does, it may lead to highly stabilized forms of behavior that are resistant to change and self-perpetuating. It is this deculturated state of affairs, affecting only a small minority of Mexican-Americans, which social scientists and lay people have equated with Mexican-American Culture.

II *Immigrant Mexican-American culture*

Particularly in the states of California and Texas, immigrant Mexican-American culture arose from the values and lifestyles of Mexican immigrants who began pouring into these regions after 1910, the year of the Mexican Revolution. Prior to this time, the indigenous Spanish/Mexican population of these regions was so small that it was quickly outnumbered and amalgamated with the new immigrants who numbered almost one million between the years 1910 and 1930. Though different in many ways, these immigrants were similar in one important respect: their motivation to leave Mexico in search of a better life for themselves and their families. This same motivation is characteristic of most Mexican immigrants today, and is therefore at the very core of immigrant Mexican-American culture both past and present.

The traditional social science view of Mexican-Americans is that they are merely "transplanted" Mexicans. According to Stoddard (1973), this misconception probably developed from early anthropological accounts of isolated Mexican villages (Redfield, 1930, 1941; Lewis, 1951) which were uncritically generalized to all of rural Mexico and in turn to Mexican immigrants who came from these areas. And, since the socioeconomic condition of these areas is so poor, many have assumed that the Mexican "character" is not suited for success. The clear implication for Mexican immigrants and their descendants is, of course, that they need to assimilate in order to achieve success.

But contrary to popular belief, the Mexican immigrant is not a "typical" Mexican. At least two lines of evidence indicate that Mexican immigrants are a highly self-selected group of individuals, a finding that has important implications for the nature of immigrant Mexican-American culture. The first line of evidence has to do with the personality makeup of Mexican immigrants relative to the rest of the Mexican population. The second set of evidence involves the educational and socioeconomic status of immigrants before coming to the United States.

Personality data come from a study by Fromm & Maccoby (1970), who sought to identify the dominant "social characters" of an entire Mexican village. Social character refers to the syndrome of personality traits that are common to most members of groups or classes within a society. According to Fromm, this syndrome of traits is important, because "the fact that they are common to most members has the result that group behavior — action, thought, feeling — is motivated by those traits which are shared" (1970, p.16). An 83-item open-ended questionnaire and a six-item short-stories test was administered to 95 percent (n=406) of the adult villagers. A sample of these villagers also took the Rorschach and Thematic Apperception Test. In addition, 92 children between the ages of 6-17 received the complete battery of tests. All scoring was done according to guidelines derived from Fromm's theory of social character (Fromm & Maccoby, 1970). Factor analysis of the data yielded three dominant social characters in the village:

1. *Receptive-Passive.* Individuals in this group are fatalistic, submissive, oriented toward fiestas, and idealize authority.
2. *Productive-Hoarding.* This group is characterized by independence, formality, responsibility, and democratic decision making.
3. *Productive-Exploitive.* The members of this group believe in progress, change, making new opportunities, mobility, and individualism (Fromm & Maccoby, 1970, p.124).

Social characters number 2 and 3 seem healthier and more suited to success and adjustment than social character number 1. What is most important about these differences in social character to the present discussion is the fact that some individuals emigrated to the United States *after* their data were collected, thereby making it possible to compare their results with those of persons who remained in Mexico. Fromm & Maccoby found a small, but significant correlation (r=.35, p < .01) between having a Productive social character (numbers 2 and 3) and going to the United States. In other words, the personalities of Mexican immigrants were more often characteristic of a Productive-Hoarding and Productive-Exploitive social character.

Further evidence of the self-selected nature of Mexican immigrants comes from studies that compare their education and occupational status to the rest of the Mexican population. Portes (1979) found that immigrants completed more years of schooling, in Mexico, than the national average for the Mexican population. In addition, the percentage of immigrants who completed primary education or had some secondary education was about double the percentage for the Mexican population.

Despite the fact that they are often stereotyped as being farmworkers, Mexican immigrants come primarily from the ranks of skilled and unskilled nonagricultural workers in Mexico. Portes (1979), for example, found that only 12 percent of the Mexican immigrants in his sample were involved in agricultural work in Mexico; the majority were skilled or semiskilled workers. Once in the United States, those immigrants who do begin their employment histories as farmworkers overwhelmingly move into nonagricultural work and also make certain that their children do not work in agriculture (Cornelius, Chavez, & Castro, 1982).

The selective nature of Mexican immigration is also described in a study by Dinerman (1982) who examined the migration patterns of two villages in Michoacan, Mexico. She notes that immigrants were more likely to come from households that: a) perceived a gap between their income levels and their desired consumption levels and b) were able to sponsor an immigrant to the United States in order to alleviate this consumption gap. In contrast, "stay-at-homes," or nonimmigrants, were more often members of households that were either so poor that they could not afford to sponsor an immigrant or so wealthy that they do not experience a consumption gap at all. Dinerman's (1982) analysis suggests that immigrants are neither the poorest nor wealthiest members of the Mexican population but rather the members of a *potential* middle class who come to the United States in order to fulfill their upwardly mobile ambitions.

Linton (1945) and others (Whiting & Child, 1953) have argued that culture creates personalities and that in turn these personalities change the culture. Following this line of reasoning, it seems logical to assume that Mexican culture gives rise to a variety of personalities, some of which are more inclined to upward mobility than others. Owing to environmental constraints against upward mobility in Mexico, individuals with more upwardly mobile personalities are more likely to emigrate than individuals with less upwardly mobile personalities. As a result, these immigrants carry with them to the United States many of the elements of Mexican culture (language, religion, foods, etc.) but, in addition, embellish these elements with their unique personalities which transforms them into immigrant Mexican-American culture. That is, since Mexican-American culture is basically a culture of immigrants, the unique personalities of this group become mapped onto the larger behavioral complex that make up their culture in the United States.

Over time, and as a result of deculturing influences, individuals may undergo changes in their behavior which in turn influence the character of Mexican-American culture. However, to the extent that individuals resist deculturation, and that immigration from Mexico continues at a steady rate, immigrant Mexican-American culture is preserved and reinforced.

III. *Empirical support for the cultural integration hypothesis*

A growing body of literature supports the hypothesis that integration with immigrant Mexican-American culture promotes success and adjustment in United States society. Tables 1, 2, and 3 summarize this research in three areas: income/occupational status; educational achievement; and avoidance of deviant behavior. With few exceptions (Buriel & Saenz, 1980; Buriel, Calzada, & Vasquez, 1982) none of the studies in Tables 1-3 intended to test the cultural integration hypothesis. In fact, some sought to demonstrate just the opposite, i.e., the damaging-culture hypothesis. Nevertheless, in all the studies cited, some indication was given of the subjects' integration with immigrant Mexican-American culture, which made it possible to test the cultural integration hypothesis. Usually, this indication was in the form of the subjects' Spanish language usage or competence and/or their generational status. Mexican-American culture arose from the values and lifestyles of Spanish-speaking Mexican immigrants. Consequently, greater Spanish language usage and competence, and earlier generational status, are reliable indicators of integration with immigrant Mexican-American culture. Individuals who are more estranged from Mexican-American culture are usually later generation and English monolingual. The validity of language and generation as markers of cultural integration has been empirically determined. Thus, Spanish usage and generational status have consistently accounted for a substantial amount of variance in scores obtained on paper-and-pencil measures of acculturation (Olmedo & Padilla, 1978; Cuellar, Harris, & Jasso, 1980; Padilla, 1980).

TABLE 1

Income/Occupational Status

Study and year	Methods	Findings
Browning and McLemore (1964)	Based on census information for Mexican Americans in the State of Texas.	Income of the second generation was "demonstrably superior" to that of the third grade.
Penalosa and McDonagh (1966)	Structured interview administered to a 6% random sample of adult Mexican Americans in Pomona, California. Mobility estimates based on occupation.	Mobility Pattern Generation Upward None Downward First 16.2% 51.6% 35.4% Second 51.2% 26.7% 22.1% Third 35.7% 28.6% 35.7%
Grebler, Moore and Guzman (1970)	Median income of Spanish surname males ages 35-44. Source: 1960 U.S. Census.	Median Income First Generation $3,682 Second Generation $4,664 Third Generation $4,454
U.S. Census (1973)	"Median income of Spanish surnamed heads of households.	Median Income First Generation $6,127 Second Generation $7,604 Third Generation $6,795
Chiswick (1979)	Re-analysis of 1970 census. Expressed annual earnings as a function of a set of explanatory variables that included years of schooling, years of labor market experience, weeks worked,	The earnings of second generation males were from 5-9 percent greater than those of third generation males. Also, after about 15 years of residence in the United States, the

TABLE 1 (continued)
Income/Occupational Status

Study and year	Methods	Findings
Chiswick (continued)	marital status, area of residence, country of birth, and number of years since immigrating to the United States.	earnings of Mexican immigrants equalled those of Mexican Americans born in this country.
Melville (1980)	Measured the rate of adaptation and social mobility aspirations of 47 Mexican American women who had recently migrated to Houston, Texas.	Only 12.5 percent of the women born in the United States held upwardly mobil aspirations compared to approximately 39 percent of the women born in the United States.
Gandara (1982)	Carried out intensive life history interviews with 17 high achieving Mexican American women who were either J.D.'s, M.D.'s or Ph.D.'s.	Seventy-seven percent were bilingual or spoke only Spanish at home, and 70 percent were born in Mexico.

TABLE 2

Educational Achievement

Study	Method	Findings
Kimball (1968)	Used grades, standardized reading tests and IQ's as measures of achievement for 899 Mexican American junior high school students.	Found significantly higher levels of achievement for students born in Mexico or with both parents born in Mexico compared with other Mexican American students.
Henderson and Merrit (1968) Henderson (1972)	Investigated the environment backgrounds of 80 Mexican American first graders with different potentials for school success. Students were from Tucson, Arizona.	Students with a high potential for school success scored higher on a test of Spanish vocabulary than the low potential group. A follow-up study of these same children at the end of the third grade confirmed that the more Spanish proficient, high potential children were doing better in school.
Cordova (1970)	Investigated the relationship of acculturation to Anglo norms to educational achievement and alienation among 477 sixth grade Spanish American students from New Mexico. Students were urban middle class, urban lower class, and rural.	For the urban middle class children, as acculturation increased achievement decreased. For all students, acculturation in the area of the family was positively correlated with alienation. That is, the more acculturated were the more alienated.

TABLE 2 (continued)

Educational Achievement

Study	Method	Findings
Cordova (continued)	Measures of acculturation and alienation were obtained from a student questionnaire. Achievement was measured by standardized tests.	

Study	Method	Findings			
Grebler, Moore and Guzman (1970)	Based on median school years completed by Spanish Surnamed persons, ages 14-24. Source: 1960 U.S. Census.	Years of school completed by percentage			
		Generation	9-11	12	Some College
		First	18.1	8.1	4.5
		Second	34.6	16.1	4.5
		Third	35.6	14.0	4.0

Study	Method	Findings		
U.S. Census (1973)	Spanish Surnamed persons living in the Southwest, ages 20-24.	Years of school completed by percentage		
		Generation	12th	Some College
		First	29.9	4.6
		Second	54.8	8.3
		Third	58.8	9.0

Study	Method	Findings
U.S. Census (1973)	15% sample of Spanish Surnamed household in the Southwest.	50% of all Chicano high school graduate and 50% of all Chicanos with 4 or more years of college reported speaking Spanish at home.
Long and Padilla (cited in Ramirez, 1971)	Compared the home language preference of Spanish surname students at the University of New	Ninety-four percent of the successful students were raised in homes were Spanish was spoken compared to

TABLE 2 (continued)
Educational Achievement

Study	Method	Findings
Long and Padilla (continued)	Mexico. Students who had successfully completed their graduate degrees were compared with those who had dropped-out of the university.	only 8 percent of the unsuccessful students.
Anderson and Johnson (1971)	Semester grades in English and Math were used to compare 163 first-, second, and third generation junior high school students who spoke varying amounts of English and Spanish at home.	Found Spanish speaking first- and second generation students to perform as well or better in both English and Math than members of the third generation who spoke greater amounts of English at home.
Schumaker and Getter (1977)	Studied the educational attainment of Mexican Americans living in 34 counties of the state of Kansas. Achievement was measured as the Median number of school years completed, and the percentage of persons over 25 years having completed high school	On all measures of achievement, the Mexican-born group excelled over the indigenous Mexican American population of the state.
Buriel and Saenz (1980)	A biculturalism questionnaire was administered to female, Mexican American	College-bound students were significantly more bicultural than their

TABLE 2 (continued)

Educational Achievement

Study	Method	Findings
Buriel and Saenz (continued)	high school seniors in Pomona, California. Students were also identified as being either college-bround or noncollege-bound on the basis of their post-graduation plans.	noncollege-bound counterparts.
Brown, Rosen, Hill and Olivas (1980)	Used data from the National Center for Education Statistics, Survey of Income and Education, Spring 1976.	Reported tht 84 percent of all Mexican Americans enrolled in college came from homes where Spanish was spoken when they were children.
Vigil and Long (1981)	Examined the high school grades of Mexican American students from southern California.	There was an inverse relationship between grades and generational status. Earlier generation students had higher grades than their later generation counterparts.
Garcia (1981)	Explored the effects of family and children's cultural maintenance upon children's achievement in college. Mexican American students from 13 colleges and universities in Texas were sampled.	Students' Spanish fluency and coming from a Spanish dominant home was positively associated with better grades in college.

TABLE 2 (continued)
Educational Achievement

Study	Method	Findings
Nielson and Fernandez (1981)	Analysis of the High School and Beyond data set compiled by the National Opinion Research Center. The Mexican-American sample included 1,068 sophomores and 1,204 seniors from throughout the country. Standardized tests were used to measure school achievement.	Although Spanish usage was associated with lower achievement, Spanish proficiency was associated with higher achievement. More importantly though, higher achievement was associated with having parents who had immigrated to the United States from Mexico.
So (1983)	Analysis of the High School and Beyond data set. Discriminant analyses performed on a group of low socioeconomic status Hispanic language minority students.	High achieving Hispanic students were more likely to have been exposed to bilingual education in grade school; use Spanish in their usual language; and, had parents who were immigrants.

TABLE 3
Avoidance of Delinquency

Study and year	Method	Findings
Darbyshire (1965)	Interviewed Mexican American adolescents from east Los Angeles. Used a values questionnaire to categorize subjects as either "Mexicanized" or "Americanized."	Mexicanized subjects placed significantly less value on the importance of belonging to a gang and also had lower arrest rates than Americanized subjects.
Jessor, Graves, Hansen and Jessor (1968)	Studied an entire tri-ethnic community in Colorado that included Native Americans, and Mexican Americans. Structured and unstructured interviews and public records were used to investigate the causes of deviancy. The study sought to test Merton's theory of legitimate access.	Found that although Mexican Americans occupied the lowest socioeconomic position in the community, their deviancy rates were as low as those of the most socioeconomically advantaged Anglo American group. This was contrary to predictions from Merton's theory. Jessor et al., attributed the lower deviancy rates of Mexican Americans to their maintenance of a strong Mexican American cultural tradition.
Moore (1978)	Carried out intensive interviews and used archival sources to study the evolution of two long standing Mexican American gangs in east Los Angeles.	Out of a total of 209 males who belonged to these two gangs between 1945 and 1960, only 3 were born in Mexico.

The studies cited in Tables 1-3 have been discussed elsewhere in length (Buriel, 1984). The following paragraphs briefly summarize their major findings.

In the area of economic and occupational success, the data generally indicate that earlier generation (usually

TABLE 3 (continued)
Avoidance of Delinquency

Study and year	Method	Findings
Vigil (1979)	Used in depth interviews to study the adaptation strategies and cultural lifestyles of Mexican American youth living in east Los Angeles. He identified three groups of adolescents: Mexican oriented; Chicano oriented; and, Anglo oriented.	Mexican oriented youths obtained better grades. Chicano oriented youths all belonged gangs. Anglo oriented youth seemed to be undergoing the most stress in their lives due to ambiguities about their identity.
Buriel and Calzada and Vasquez (1982)	Studied male Mexican American high students from southern California. Students' educational aspirations, expectations and their self reported levels of deviancy were measured. First-, second-, and third generation students were sampled.	There was no difference in the educational aspirations of the three groups. However, third generation students had lower educational expectations and higher deviancy rates than either first- or second generation students who did not differ from each other.

the first and second) workers and heads of household do better than their later generation (usually third or later) counterparts. This finding is all the more impressive considering that most immigrants have fewer job skills (years of education and English fluency) when entering the labor market than native-born Mexican-Americans. Melville (1980) and Gandara's (1982) studies also dispel the myth of the passive Mexican-American female while at the same time revealing that greater achievement among women is positively related to integration with immigrant Mexican-American culture.

While the overall educational attainment of the Mexican-American population is modest, there are some important within-group differences indicating that higher achieving individuals tend to be earlier

generation and fluent Spanish speakers. The earliest
information concerning within-group differences comes
from census reports. These data show mixed results. In
1960 the educational attainment of the more traditional
second generation outpaced that of the third generation,
while in 1970 there was practically no difference
between these two groups. Consistently though, the first
generation had the fewest high school graduates. This
is to be expected since most immigrants come to this
country as young adults who are already beyond the
normal high school age.

Perhaps historical events intervening between 1960
and 1970 help to explain the mixed census results for
these two time periods. The cultural pride awakened by
the Chicano Movement during the 1960s may have
encouraged many later generation Mexican-Americans
to strengthen their ties with their ancestral culture and
as a result boosted their educational attainment. Thus
by 1970 there was no longer a difference in educational
attainment between the second and third generation. Of
course, we cannot be certain about the accuracy of this
explanation. Nevertheless, it does seem consistent with
the finding that in 1970, according to the census, half of
all Mexican-American high school graduates, and 48
percent of all college graduates, reported speaking
Spanish at home (United States Bureau of the Census,
1973).

It must be noted that serious doubts have been cast on
the validity of the 1970 census for Mexican-Americans
because of deficient methodological procedures used in
enumerating persons from Spanish-speaking
backgrounds (United States Civil Rights Commission,
1974). And unfortunately, the 1980 census is not broken
down in sufficient detail to permit relevant analyses by
either generation or language. At present, therefore, our
most reliable information concerning within-group
differences in educational achievement comes from
individual studies conducted in different parts of the
country. These individual studies are the remaining
entries in Table 2.

A perusal of Table 2 reveals that, consistent with the
cultural integration hypothesis, earlier generational

status and Spanish language usage and proficiency are positively related to higher educational achievement. Collectively, these individual studies seem fairly representative of the Mexican-American population, inasmuch as they involved age groups ranging from first grade through college and diverse geographical areas, including California, Arizona, Texas, New Mexico, and Kansas. But perhaps the most compelling evidence in favor of the cultural integration hypothesis comes from the High School and Beyond Study (Nielson & Fernandez, 1981) which sampled over 2,000 Mexican-descent students from across the country. Multiple regression analyses of that large data set have revealed that educational achievement is higher among students who are proficient in Spanish and who came from immigrant families.

In her widely cited book, *Mexican-American Youth: Forgotten Youth at the Crossroads,* Heller (1966) stated that "the excess of juvenile delinquents among Mexican-Americans...is not composed of deviants from the cultural pattern but rather of boys who over conform to this pattern" (p. 76). Heller's remarks clearly reflect the logic of the damaging-culture model since she assumes that those individuals who are most integrated in Mexican-American culture are also the ones who are most damaged, in this case, the most delinquent. The available research, however, does not support Heller's assumption. Inspection of Table 3 reveals that lower levels of delinquent behavior are consistently associated with variables that mark greater integration with immigrant Mexican-American culture: earlier generational status and identification with traditional values.

One study in particular sought to determine the validity of the cultural integration hypothesis for explaining within-group differences in juvenile delinquency. In that study, Buriel, Calzada, & Vasquez (1982) sampled first, second, and third generation male adolescents and collected information on their educational aspirations, expectations, and involvement in delinquent behaviors. Since previous research had shown that aspiration-expectation disjunctions create pressures toward deviancy, it was hypothesized that third generation males would have the largest disjunctions and that in turn these would be positively correlated to a higher rate of delinquency for members of this group. Results showed that third generation males had greater disjunctions and higher deviancy scores than either first or second generation subjects. In addition, the disjunction between aspirations and expectations was positively correlated to delinquency for the third generation. The findings indicated that third generation Mexican-Americans more often felt less capable of achieving their education aspirations and that this may have contributed to more pressures toward deviancy which was reflected in their higher delinquency scores. Since first and second generation males were socialized by immigrant parents, they were more likely to be influenced by immigrant Mexican-American culture than their third generation peers. Owing to the achievement oriented nature of immigrant Mexican-American culture, first and second generation adolescents may have been socialized with higher expectations for success that in turn offset pressures toward deviancy.

III Conclusion

Throughout the Southwest, and particularly in California, there is an ever increasing shortage of teachers. As new teachers enter the profession, they will inevitably be required to instruct a growing number of Mexican-American pupils representing children of foreign- and native-born families. Teacher credentialing programs should instruct teacher candidates about the diversity of the Mexican-American population in order to dispel inaccurate stereotypes and create higher teacher expectations. Working under the assumption that assimilation is desirable for Mexican immigrants, teachers may overlook the achievement oriented characteristics of immigrants that are conducive to success in this society. Teachers therefore need to recognize and appreciate the achievement potential inherent in immigrant Mexican-American culture and to use this knowledge to promote the academic performance of all Mexican-descent students.

REFERENCES

Anderson, J.G., & Johnson, W.H. Stability and change among three generations of Mexican-Americans: Factors affecting achievement. *American Educational Research Journal.* 1971, *8,* 285-309.

Barry, J.W. Acculturation as varieties of adaptation. In A.M. Padilla (Ed.), *Acculturation: theory, models and some new findings.* Boulder, Colo.: Westview Press, 1980.

Brown, G.H., Rosen, N.L., Hill, S.T., & Olivas, M.A. *The condition of education for Hispanic Americans.* Washington, D.C.: National Center for Educational Statistics, 1980.

Browning, H.L., & McLemore, S.D. *A statistical profile of the Spanish-surname population of Texas.* Austin: Bureau of Business Research, 1964.

Buriel, R. Integration with traditional Mexican-American culture and sociocultural adjustment. In J.L. Martinez and R. Mendoza (Eds.), *Chicano Psychology* (2nd ed.). New York: Academic Press, 1984.

Buriel, R., Calzada, S., & Vasquez, R. The relationship of traditional Mexican-American culture to adjustment and delinquency among three generations of Mexican-American adolescents. *Hispanic Journal of Behavioral Sciences,* 1982, *4,* 41-55.

Buriel, R., & Saenz, E. Psychocultural characteristics of college bound and non-college bound Chicanas. *Journal of Social Psychology,* 1980, *110,* 245-251.

Chiswick, B.R. The economic progress of immigrants: Some apparently universal patterns. In W. Fellner (Ed.), *Contemporary economic problems 1979.* Washington, D.C.: American Enterprise Institute, 1979.

Cordova, I.R. The relationship of acculturation, achievement, and alienation among Spanish-American sixth grade students. In H.S. Johnson & W.J. Hernandez (Eds.), *Educating the Mexican American,* Valley Forge, Pa.: Judson Press, 1970.

Cornelius, W.A., Chavez, L.R., & Castro, J.G. Mexican immigrants and southern California: A summary of current knowledge. *Working papers in U.S.-Mexican Studies.* No. 36. La Jolla, Calif.: Center for U.S.-Mexican Studies, University of California, San Diego, 1982.

Cuellar, I., Harris, L.C., & Jasso, R. An acculturation scale for Mexican-American normal and clinical populations. *Hispanic Journal of Behavioral Sciences,* 1980, *2,* 199-217.

Demos, G.D. Attitudes of Mexican-American and Anglo-American groups toward education. *Journal of Social Psychology,* 1962, *57,* 249-256.

Derbyshire, R.L. Adolescent identity crisis in urban Mexican-Americans in East Los Angeles. In E.B. Brody (Ed.), *Minority group Adolescents in the United States.* Baltimore: The Williams and Wilkins Company, 1968.

Dinerman, I.R. Migrants and stay-at-homes: A comparative study of rural migration from Michoacan, Mexico. Monography series, 5. Center for U.S.-Mexico Studies, University of California, San Diego, 1982.

Fromm, E., & Maccoby, M. *Social character in a Mexican village.* Englewood Cliffs, N.J.: Prentice-Hall, 1970.

Gamio, Manuel. *The Mexican immigrant: His life-story.* Chicago: Ill.: University of Chicago Press, 1931.

Gandara, P. Passing through the eye of the needle. High-achieving Chicanas. *Hispanic Journal of Behavioral Sciences,* 1982, *4,* 167-179.

Garcia, H.D.C. *Bilingualism, confidence, and college achievement* (Report No. 318). Center for Social Organization of Schools, The Johns Hopkins University, Baltimore, Md.: 1981.

Gordon, M.M. *Assimilation in American Life.* New York: Oxford, University Press, 1964.

Grebler, L., Moore, J.W. & Guzman, R.C. *The Mexican-American people: The nation's second largest minority.* New York: The Free Press, 1970.

Heller, C. *Mexican-American Youth: Forgotten youth at the crossroads.* New York: Random House, 1966.

Henderson, R.W. Environmental predictors of academic performance of disadvantaged Mexican-American children. *Journal of Consulting and Clinical Psychology,* 1972, *38,* 297.

Henderson, R.W. Environmental predictors of academic performance of disadvantaged Mexican-American children. *Journal of Consulting and Clinical Psychology,* 1972, *38,* 297.

Henderson, R.W., & Merritt, C.G. Environmental backgrounds of Mexican-American children with different potentials for school success. *Journal of Social Psychology,* 1968, 75-101-106.

Jessor, R., Graves, T.D., Hansen, R.C., & Jessor, S.L., *Society, personality, and deviant behavior: A study of a tri-ethnic community.* New York: Holt, Rinehart & Winston, 1968.

Kimball, W.L. Parent and family influence on academic achievement among Mexican-American students (Doctoral dissertation, University of California, Los Angeles, 1968). *Dissertation Abstracts International,* 1968, 29, 1965A (University Microfilms, No. 68-16, 550).

Kuvlesky, W.P., & Patella, V.M. Degree of ethnicity and aspirations for upward mobility among Mexican-American youth. *Journal of Vocational Behavior,* 1971, *1,* 231-244.

Lewis, O. *Teopoztlan restudied: Life in a Mexican village.* Urbana: University of Illinois Press, 1951.

Linton, R. *The cultural background of personality.* New York: Appleton-Century-Crofts, 1945.

Melville, M.B. Selective acculturation of female Mexican immigrants. In M.B. Melville (Ed.), *Twice a minority: Mexican-American women.* Saint Louis, Mo.: The V.C. Mosby Company, 1980.

Moore, J. W. *Homeboys.* Philadelphia: Temple University Press, 1978.

Nielson, F., & Fernandez, R.M. *Hispanic students in American high schools: Background characteristics and achievement.* National Center for Education Statistics. Washington, D.C.: U.S. Government Printing Office, 1981.

Olmedo, E.L., & Padilla, A.M. Empirical and construct validation of a measure of acculturation for Mexican-Americans. *Journal of Social Psychology,* 1978, *105,* 179-187.

Padilla, A.M. The role of cultural awareness and ethnic loyalty in acculturation. In A.M. Padilla (Ed.), *Acculturation: Theory models, and some new findings.* Boulder, Colo.: Westview Press, 1980.

Penalosa, F., & McDonagh, E.C. Social mobility in a Mexican-American community. *Social Forces,* 1966, *44,* 498-505.

Portes. Illegal immigration and the international system: Lessons from recent legal Mexican immigration to the United States. *Social Problems,* 1979, 26, *4,* April, p. 425.

Ramirez, M. The relationship of acculturation to educational achievement and psychological adjustment in Chicano children and adolescents: A review of the literature. *El Grito: A Journal of contemporary Mexican-American thought,* 1971, *4,* 21-28.

Ramirez, M., & Castaneda, A. *Cultural democracy, bicognitive developmental education.* New York: Academic Press, 1974.

Redfield, R. *Tepoztlan: A Mexican Village.* Chicago: University of Chicago Press, 1930.

Redfield, R. *The folk culture of Yucatan.* Chicago: University of Chicago Press, 1941.

Schumaker, P.D., & Getter, R.W. The community bases of minority educational attainment. *Journal of Education,* 1977, 159, 5-22.

So, A.Y. The analysis of language minority issues in national data sets. *La Red/The Net.* No. 71, August 1983.

Stoddard, E.R. *Mexican-Americans.* New York: Random House, 1973.

United States Bureau of the Census. Census of Population: 1970. Subject Reports, PC (2) — 1D, *Persons of Spanish Surname,* Washington, D.C.: United States Government Printing Office, 1973.

United States Civil Rights Commission. *Counting the Forgotten,* Washington, D.C.: U.S. Government Printing Office, April 1974.

Vigil, D. Adaptation strategies and cultural life styles of Mexican adolescents. *Hispanic Journal of Behavioral Sciences,* 1979, *1,* 375-392.

Vigil, J.D., & Long, J.M. Undirectional or nativist acculturation — Chicano paths to school achievement. *Human Organization,* 1981, *40,* 273-277.

Whiting, J.W., & Child, I.L. *Child training and personality: A cross-cultural study.* New Haven, Conn.: Yale University Press, 1953.

Hidden Resources in the Reading and Writing of Bilingual Children

Paul Ammon and Mary Sue Ammon

We are concerned in this paper with bilingual children who are learning English as a second language at the same time they are learning to read and write. More specifically, we are concerned with their progress in learning to read and write in English. Rather than discuss the literacy development of all bilingual children as a group, however, we wish to look closely at a few bilingual children as individuals.

To begin seeing how the kind of close-up view we have in mind differs from a more distant, global view, let us imagine that we are gradually zooming in on the population of bilingual children from a considerable distance. At first, the only thing we see is that the group as a whole is not doing very well in English reading and writing. Then, as we start getting closer, we begin to notice that there is a wide range of individual differences within the group. Some students are rapidly overtaking many of their native English-speaking peers in their control over written English, while others seem to have made little progress in that direction so far. And, of course, many students fall somewhere in between. If we look even closer at these in-between students, we can see that they are not distributed neatly along a single continuum of progress toward mature reading and writing in English, because many of them show varying and sometimes striking mixtures of strengths and weaknesses in their reading and writing. Finally, if we were taking time-lapse motion pictures of these individuals (as opposed to single snapshots), we might see evidence of growth spurts, plateaus, and even regressions, and all of these might be happening simultaneously with respect to different aspects of the same student's literacy development.

In choosing to look closely at such performance patterns, our goal is to uncover clues as to a given individual's resources for English reading and writing at a particular point in time, and to use these clues as a basis for discussing how teachers might proceed in helping students use their resources to move forward toward more effective reading and writing. We are also looking for lessons we might learn from bilingual children that could enhance our understanding of how other children learn to read and write as well.

With many specialists in cognitive science we share the view that reading and writing are complex problem-solving activities. With specialists in the study of development we share the view that learning to read and write is a constructive process that arises from the child's efforts to deal with the problems posed by reading and writing. Variations in background and in classroom learning environments can help or hinder this process, but the ultimate source of progress in learning to read and write is the child's own problem-solving activity. That is why we thought it important to see what the individual children in our study were actually *doing* in their reading and writing — to see how they were dealing with the problems posed by specific reading and writing tasks.

Background

During the 1981-82 school year, we participated in a large study commissioned by the National Institute of Education to investigate the acquisition of school-related English language skills by children who were learning English as a second language. (1) The chief purposes of the study were to identify instructional practices that were particularly effective in promoting the acquisition of the English language skills in question, and to see how particular learner characteristics interacted with different learning situations to affect language learning outcomes. Because the data have not yet been completely analyzed, the jury is still out on the question of effective instructional practices. However, it is clear to us by now that the data provide unusual opportunities for exploring the reading and writing performance patterns of individual children across different situations, and for considering their educational implications, which is what we aim to do here.

The principal body of data for the larger study came from a total of 157 children, who varied in a number of ways. Some were third graders and some were fifth graders. Some spoke Spanish as their first language and some spoke Cantonese. And they varied in many other ways as well, such as the extent to which English was spoken in their homes, or whether they were born in the U.S. or elsewhere. However, all of the children had had two to three years' prior exposure to English in school, and all had been identified as Limited English Proficiency students by their schools. The children came from 17 different classrooms, and these varied also. Some of them were designated as bilingual classrooms, in that instruction was sometimes carried out in the children's first language. In other classrooms, the only language of instruction was English. And, of course, the classrooms differed in a number of other ways too, including the ethnic diversity of the students and the manner in which the teachers approached instruction. It seems likely that a consideration of these classroom variables, along with the background variables mentioned above, will eventually inform our understanding of the individual performance patterns we have observed. But we wish to keep the focus here on the patterns themselves and on what they might tell us about the children's resources for reading and writing.

Procedures

In order to test reading comprehension at a level of difficulty appropriate for each subject, and to provide a standardized measure of proficiency like that obtained by schools in their testing programs, a screening test consisting of two subtests from a standardized test battery (auditory vocabulary and word reading) and a Spanish or Cantonese auditory vocabulary test was administered to the students during the first weeks of the school year. In the individually administered pretest of reading comprehension that followed the screening test, each child received four different passages to read. Each paragraph was followed by a set of multiple-choice questions designed to test comprehension. Children read the first paragraph aloud, and this oral reading was timed; miscues were recorded and subsequently classified qualitatively. The second paragraph was read silently. After answering written questions for these two passages, children were asked the reasons for their selection of each answer. The third paragraph was also read silently. After responding to the written questions, each child was asked to reread the passage and then to retell the story orally. Examiners then probed for memory and understanding of points inadequately covered in the summarization. Finally, the fourth paragraph was presented according to a procedure developed by Fillmore and Kay (2), in which the text is exposed one sentence or phrase at a time and children are asked questions about their evolving understanding or envisionment of the text after reading aloud each succeeding piece.

An important aspect of the reading tasks that were administered was that they were designed to provide information about the process as well as the products of reading. So we collected reading "product" data on speed of decoding, the number of major and minor decoding errors, vocabulary scores in English and L1, the number of correct responses on word reading and reading comprehension tasks, and the extent to which basic content was recalled in story summarizations. But we also recorded the type of incorrect reading comprehension responses, the justifications for these choices, the relation of these responses to story summarizations, and the students' ability to interpret different sources of information in texts, to understand the story, and to change their envisionments when confronted with subsequent information or problematic questions.

Samples of student writing were elicited in individual interviews by means of standard picture prompts and instructions. There were two kinds of writing tasks — stories and comparative descriptions. Before writing, the children were asked to tell the interviewer what they planned to write. If they seemed to be having trouble interpreting the pictures, they were asked questions to guide their perceptions of what the pictures showed.

Each of the writing samples collected in this way was rated from 1 to 5 on several dimensions, including completeness and elaboration of content, sense of genre, clarity of reference, cohesion, and use of conventional spelling and grammar. Each dimension was intended to represent a different aspect of writing that might determine how clearly a given piece would communicate to readers who were not already familiar with the writer or the topic. The writing scores we will refer to below were based on the sum of these dimension ratings.

Some individual patterns of reading and writing performance

Our investigations to date have made us more and more wary of drawing conclusions about a child's resources for dealing with written English from a single instance of reading or writing performance. It is not unusual for important resources to remain hidden from view on any one occasion — even resources that are directly relevant to the task at hand. Consider the example of Maria, a third grader, who began her story about a purse-snatching incident with the words, "The men gat the prrs..." Unlike some of the other students we have seen, Maria provides no evidence here that she knows how to frame a story by means of an opening which introduces characters and establishes a setting. However, when she wrote the same story in Spanish, she began, "Un dia una sejora (senora)..." [One day a lady...]. In other words, Maria *did* know how to frame a story but did not do so when writing in English — probably because the extra burden of writing in a new language led her to focus exclusively on the basic essentials of the story. (3)

This example illustrates an obvious point: the way bilingual children perform in their first languages can be a valuable source of information about their resources for becoming literate in English. But many teachers who work with bilingual students are not in a position to make use of such first-language data, and it seems to us that a great deal can be learned about a child's resources just by looking closely at a variety of reading and writing performances in English, so that is the approach we will pursue here.

The validity of this approach is supported by some data we have on Maria's English reading, which again show the difficulty she has with written representations of English, but also give further evidence of her well developed sense of the story genre. Maria labored long and painfully on the first oral reading paragraph, taking almost seven minutes to read 53 words and making 13 serious decoding errors. But when it came to summarizing and answering comprehension questions, her ability to make sense of stories was truly surprising, especially considering the number of gaps in the story she had to fill. (See her retelling of the "Overboard" story in Figure 1.) Certainly Maria's strength in making sense of stories should stand her in good stead as she acquires more decoding skill. Her case also illustrates the point that children of low decoding ability need not and should not be relegated to lessons which focus exclusively on the development of low-level decoding skills. Teaching to Maria's strengths would mean allowing her to engage in more integrative literacy activities such as discussing stories and constructing original stories, even before she has the skill to read much interesting text without help.

Figure 1
Maria's Retelling of "Overboard" Story

Story Presented:

A man fell into the water. He was about to go under when a big turtle came up to him. The man held onto the turtle all night long. The next day they were seen by a ship. The turtle had saved the man.

Maria's Retelling:

A man fell into the water, and then the man were able to go under the water. Then the turtle went up to him...and the turtle helped him and then he couldn't drowned. And then the turtle he stay under

the water for...night long. The next morning they
saw a ship cause they lift up their head. And they
saw a ship, so they went by him and then these
men helped the man. And the turtle stayed under
the water.

Another third grader, Luong, seemed to be somewhat
further along than Maria in gaining control over
written English, but his performances in English were
still more or less average among our bilingual subjects
— except in one area that is illustrated by Figure 2. The
story Luong wrote about the purse-snatching episode
received a score that was 2.2 standard deviations above
the mean for all of our third graders. Despite a few
problems with English grammar and spelling, the story
is outstanding not only for its complete coverage of
basic story content, but also for its elaboration on why
and how characters did what they did. In terms of form,
it shows clarity of reference, use of cohesive ties such as
anaphora and ellipsis, and a good sense of the story
genre. In fact, the story genre seemed to be Luong's
particular strength, as he did not perform nearly as well
on the more expository descriptive writing tasks.
Luong's superior story production ability was also
evident in our reading data, where his retellings of
stories he had read stood out above other aspects of his
reading. If one had looked only at Luong's decoding
ability, or at his ability to write expository prose, his
resources for producing good stories would have
remained hidden.

Figure 2
Luong's Narrative Writing Sample

One day there was a lady name Jenny her hat was
dirty She wanted to wash it but she can't so she
went to the hat store and she look at the window
and there came a roboer and wanted to steal her
pruse and he did and than he ran. One man that
sitting and waiting for the bus to come he saw
Jenny call Help! And he saw the man that running
with a pruse he think that must be a rober and
than he take his stick and make the rober fall down
and dropped the pruse the man was good he help
her get back her pruse of moneys and he call fast

who evers you are call the polle and she did with a
phound and the polle help him She got the bad and
mean rober and the man help her get back her
pruse and than Jenny was so hanny she said thank
you very much.

The End

Because our approach entailed taking a
developmental as well as a cognitive perspective on
what students were accomplishing in their reading and
writing, we were particularly interested in discovering
students' relative strengths and weaknesses, and the
extent to which they were adopting partially adequate,
incomplete, or perhaps maladaptive strategies in
reading and writing. Thus instead of looking just at
total scores on, for example, the reading comprehension
test (i.e., the number of wrong or right answers), we
concentrated on looking for *patterns* of errors that
might reveal particular strategies or skill deficiencies.
Mei Ling and Yuen were third graders who represented
students in two distinct groups that we identified. Like
the others in these two groups, both of them had
English vocabulary scores that were very low in
comparison to their Cantonese vocabulary scores, and
both had adopted extreme (but different) strategies for
answering comprehension questions. Mei Ling, like
others in her group, almost exclusively used a strategy
of trying to find words in the text that matched words in
the answer alternatives on the comprehension test. For
example, for a comprehension test item like that
displayed in Figure 3, she would choose the second
answer alternative, "in the front of the classroom."

Figure 3
Example of Reading Test Item with Distractors Attractive to Readers Using "Matching Words" or "Associational" Strategies*

Story Excerpt: The teacher asked Bill and Bob to
roll the book cart to the front of the room...They
pushed the cart as hard as they could, but it didn't
move.

Question: Where was the book cart?

a. in the library
b. in the front of the classroom
c. in the hallway
d. in the back of the classroom

---

*Item was taken from the Stanford Diagnostic Reading Test, Green Level, 1976 edition.

On the story retelling task, she seemed to be stringing together memorized words and phrases (see Figure 4).

Figure 4
Mei Ling's Retelling of "Blue Egg" Story

*Story Presented:**

Pat noticed it at the last possible moment. It was good that she had, because she had almost stepped on it. It was the most beautiful shade of blue she had ever seen. Pat decided that it must have fallen out of one of the nests in the tree above. She bent down to look at it and saw that it had not broken. "Oh good," she thought. "Maybe if I leave it alone, it will still hatch.

Mei Ling's Retelling:

Pat notice the last possible moment that she seen... when Pat walk she saw a nest that is fallen down and step on it... and bend down and look.
[What did she see?]
It was not broken.
[What will she do?]
I will leave it alone. Maybe it will get hitch.

---

*Story was taken from the Stanford Diagnostic Reading Test, Green Level, 1976 edition.

In contrast, Yuen and the others in her group tended to over rely on their own background knowledge, associations, and intuitions when answering the comprehension questions, choosing answers such as the "in the library" alternative in Figure 3 when asked where the book cart was, and then explaining, "Because in the library many book... library have many book." It seems possible that both of these opposite tendencies — i.e., either to over accommodate to the text or over assimilate the story content to personal experiences and associations — may have arisen from these students' meager grasp of the English lexicon. Thus knowing the meaning of too few English words might have left these children with little choice but to memorize and match surface phrases *or* to over rely on their own background knowledge. And though a knowledge gap in English vocabulary might have led to the adoption of these extreme strategies (with perhaps individual personality or style mediating the particular strategy selected), it is also possible that the students' use of the strategies was interfering with their progress in learning the meanings of new words from context, thus prolonging their problems with English reading.

A different problem that emerged in a third group of Chinese students was a relatively low level of application of metacognitive knowledge about stories, reading, and reading tests. David, a third grader in this group, seemed unable to reflect on the reasons for his comprehension test choices, seemed unaware that he could reread a text if he could not remember a piece of information, dealt with sentences in isolation rather than producing or trying to understand connected text, and seemed to be lacking an organizing schema for stories. As can be seen from Figure 5, David's story retelling consists of a series of unattributed quotes that were not integrated into a narrative framework. Though David's *writing* scores showed substantial gains from the fall to the spring of the year, his written narratives, like his oral story retellings, showed little overall organization, consisting primarily of lists of activities or descriptions of individual pictures. (4)

Figure 5
David's Retelling of "Missing Cat" Story

Story Presented:*

"Where's the cat?" dad asked. "We can't leave until we take him next door to stay with the Kaplans." "Tink was on the porch," answered Jess. "On the porch!" dad said, frowning. "Jess, I asked you to keep the porch door locked. That cat pushes against the unlocked door and swings it open. Then he disappears for the day." "I did lock the door, dad,"

Jess said. Mother shouted, "Don't blame Jess! Our suitcases were piled in the hall, and you carried them to the car. You left the porch door open between trips to the car." "So I did," dad said, "and I'm sorry, Jess." Suddenly they heard a noise from the car. "I think I know where Tink is hiding," Jess said.

David's Retelling:

"Where's the cat? We can't leave until we find the cat. I told you to lock the door." [Who said that?] Dad. "I did lock the door. Don't bang the suitcase." [Who said that?] Mother...mother shouted...[Who did Dad blame for the cat being gone?] "Sorry." [When Dad couldn't find the cat, Dad blamed someone. Who did Dad blame?] Jess. [Why?] Because Jess didn't lock the door. [So what happened then?] The cat went out. [And what really happened. How did the cat get out?] Jess forgot to lock the door and then the cat pushed the door open.

---

*Story was taken from the SRA Achievement Test, Level D, Form 1.

Some of the performance problems we see in children's reading and writing seem to result not from knowledge gaps or from the overuse of some strategy, but from "growth errors" that are a natural part of development. Resources a child already appears to have may disappear from view, temporarily, as the child tries to do something new, either because the child lacks the wherewithal, at least initially, to do new things *and* old ones at the same time or because new ways of reading or writing are overgeneralized to situations where old ways would be more appropriate.

The posttest writing samples of a third-grade student, Marvin, provide an interesting example of how progress in literacy skills may not always be obvious, because a student is attempting more ambitious things and has not yet worked out how to do them well. Marvin, like the previously discussed David, was in the group of Chinese students who were identified as having problems with their ability to use general organizational strategies, especially in generating or understanding stories. But whereas David made substantial gains in his writing scores, especially for descriptions, Marvin showed substantial losses from the fall to the spring testing. However, a closer examination of Marvin's posttest narrative writing sample (especially in relation to that of David) suggests that Marvin had made clear gains in trying to incorporate more content, construct more structurally complex utterances, and create an overall organizing structure for his narratives. Whereas David used only simple sentences and sentences coordinated with "and," Marvin used complex sentences with adverbial and relative clauses to foreground the activities of the big boy and girl and to generate an overall perspective for the story (see Figure 6). He also employed shifts in tense and aspect markers to mark the main story line events (changing from "was building" for the initial background activities of the little boy and girl to "came," "ran," and "crash through"). Another interesting thing to note is that he elaborated the end of the story a little to provide a more definite conclusion. What we are suggesting is that Marvin's attention to these matters may have interfered with the coherence of his writing (resulting in lower overall writing scores), but that there are many signs that he was, in fact, making progress toward more mature writing in English.

Figure 6
Posttest Narrative Writing Samples
Produced by David and Marvin

David:

there are two children are makeing a cales and there are two children are riding a bike. And the boy nock the blocks down. And the girl say pick the block back. And the girl pick the chiddren up. and the boy put the block back.

Marvin:

When the little boy and Girl was building a house a boy came with his bike ran toaward the boy and Girl The boy crash threw the house and when the boy stop his bike and look at them When the woman went on the grass She saw the boy and girl was laying on thier knee and She Stop too So She picked up the girl and the boy and She hugg theml

and the boy who broke the house He is building
back the house When the boy finish putting back
the peace When the boy who crash the house so he
fixed back and the woman said goodby too the Kids
and the man looked at the Kids and the Kids
smiled at the woman and the man. So the man and
woman went back too thier own home.

A particularly striking example of development
causing performance problems comes from a third
grader named Lee. A comparison of her total writing
scores in the fall and spring suggests that there was
little improvement during the year. However, when her
scores for narrative and descriptive writing are
examined separately, we find that the former went up
while the latter went down. A look at Lee's writing
samples provides an explanation. In the fall, she
essentially just described what was shown in each of
the pictures we used to elicit both kinds of writing. This
strategy served her well enough in the descriptive task,
but not in the narrative task, because what she wrote
there had none of the trappings of a story. In the spring,
her response to the narrative task was much more
obviously a story, but she also tried — inappropriately
— to write a story in response to the descriptive task,
thereby lowering her score for description. Presumably
her ability to write descriptive prose was at least as well
developed as it had been before, but it was obscured now
by her newly developed and overgeneralized ability to
write stories.

Like Lee, another third grader, named Cheryl, also
showed a distinct drop from fall to spring in her score
for descriptive writing. In this case, however, the drop
seems to have resulted from Cheryl's attempt to do
something more advanced and more difficult within the
description genre itself. In the fall she began a
comparison of two kinds of fish by describing some
differences between them, but in the spring, when
writing about two kinds of birds, she focused initially on
their similarities (see Figure 7). The latter strategy
seems more advanced because it establishes some
commonalities as a context for discussing differences.
However, it is also more difficult, because the writer

must explicitly introduce each kind of bird, even though the first order of business is to say what "they" have in common, and because the writer must discriminate between features that *they* have in common and features that *all* birds have in common, which necessitates a mental comparison between the two kinds of birds in the picture and what the writer knows about birds in general. Both requirements of the more advanced strategy caused problems for Cheryl when she attempted to use it in her piece on birds. She did not tell the reader what she was describing, and she cited some features that are common to all birds. Consequently, her score dropped, masking the fact that she *could* be both clearer and more informative in her descriptive writing.

Figure 7
Excerpts from Cheryl's Descriptive Writing

Comparison of fish:
The Bay fish are up [i.e, swim near the surface] and the Ocean fish are down [swim near the bottom]. The Ocean fish is eat the grass and the Bay fish is eat the small fash [i.e., fish]...

Comparison of birds:
They all have a nest. They all have eggs. They all have a tail...

Our final example is of interest because, unlike the last two, the student's writing scores showed a gain in description but a drop in narration. Ruben included more concrete detail in his spring description than in the fall, but it was a *lack* of such detail that caused his story score to go down. In his spring story, Ruben seemed less concerned with what the characters actually did than with their feelings and intentions. This selective attention to the psychological states of characters can be seen as a sign of development on Ruben's part, or as the result of a personal disposition to be interested in such things — a disposition that was engaged more strongly by the pictures used to elicit the spring story than by those used in the fall. In any case, Ruben's ability to describe the actions in a narrative was at least partially hidden, because his attention had been drawn elsewhere. Writing in detail about both action *and* psychological states may still have been too difficult for him when he was writing in English, his second language.

Conclusion

What, then, are the implications of these individual performance patterns? What meaning do they have for educators? One answer to this question comes from a traditional diagnosis-and-remediation perspective. It is that an individual student's profile can show us areas of weakness which should be targeted for instruction. We have seen evidence in our data, for example, that some children seemed ready to make rapid progress if they were given opportunities to improve their English vocabularies or their decoding skills in reading.

The diagnosis-and-remediation perspective is a useful one, but it also has some pitfalls. For one thing, it may lead us to engage children in learning activities that are aimed *only* at their weaknesses and that do not allow them to use and improve their strengths. Another pitfall is that we may aim our instruction at deficiencies that do not really exist. As we have seen, children's resources are not always manifest in their performances.

To avoid these pitfalls, it seems important that we try to identify strengths as well as weaknesses. Indeed, it is arguable that allowing students to pursue their strengths is the key to remediating their weaknesses. However, the identification of a child's strengths may be something less than straightforward, due to the phenomenon of hidden resources.

We have seen that a child's current resources can be hidden from view for a number of reasons. Understanding these possible reasons may help us find the resources that are there. One possibility is that the child may possess resources which are simply not relevant to the task at hand, or at least are not perceived as such. Another possibility is that the use of relevant resources is preempted by the strong activation of less appropriate resources, or of relevant resources that monopolize the child's attention. And sometimes the use of available resources may be contingent on other resources that are *not* available to the child as yet. All of these possibilities are known to occur in other domains of development. Exactly how they are realized in a bilingual child's reading and writing performance will depend not only on development but on the individual's background, immediate experience, and other personal characteristics as well.

These considerations have a number of implications for both teachers and researchers. First, they point up the value of looking at performance in detail across a variety of tasks. Second, they suggest that it is also important to look at performance over time. And, third, they indicate the need to assess and respond to students on an individual basis. For classroom teachers, this does not necessarily imply a heavy emphasis on one-on-one instruction, which often seems desirable but is not always feasible. It does suggest, however, that teachers should involve students in a variety of activities that are both rich and flexible enough for individual students to utilize and further develop the full range of relevant resources at their disposal.

To help teachers in this endeavor, there is a need for more research investigating individual children's performance patterns in depth and seeing how they change over time and in response to particular kinds of experiences. Research along these lines with bilingual students may also shed light on the manner in which *all* children learn to read and write. It seems likely that virtually all of the phenomena we have examined here can be found, perhaps in subtler forms, among children learning to read and write in their native languages. The ups and downs in the performance profiles of bilingual children, and the changes that occur in them over time, may be more dramatic than for other children, because their bilingualism and their varied backgrounds create more marked and varied disparities among the resources they have in different areas. But the same kinds of variability probably occur in other children as well, albeit to a lesser extent. Thus research on bilingual children may give us a special window on reading and writing development in general, in addition to providing a more adequate basis for helping such children learn to read and write in a new language.

REFERENCES

1 Wong Fillmore, L., Ammon, P., Ammon, M.S., Delucchi, K., Jensen, J., McLaughlin, B., & Strong, M. (1983, May). *Learning English through bilingual instruction: Second year report.* (Contract: 400-80-0030). Washington, D.C.: National Instititute of Education.

2 Fillmore, C.J. (1982). Ideal readers and real readers. In D. Tannen (Ed.), *Analyzing discourse: Text and talk.* (Thirty-second round table monograph on language and linguistics, pp. 248-270). Washington, D.C.: Georgetown University Press.

  Fillmore, C. J., & Kay, P. (1981). *Text semantic analysis of reading comprehension tests.* Progress report (NIE Project 9-0511).

  Fillmore, C. J. & Kay, P. (1983, August). *Text semantic analysis of reading comprehension tests.* (Report No. G-790121). Washington, D.C.: National Institute of Education.

3 Ammon, P. (1985). Helping children learn to write in English as a second language: Some observations and some hypotheses. In S.W. Freedman (Ed.), *The acquisition of written language: Response and revision.* Norwood, N.J.: Ablex.

4 Ammon, M.S. (in press). Patterns of performance among bilingual children who score low in reading. In S. Goldman & H. Trueba (Eds.), *Becoming literate in English as a second language.* Norwood, N.J.: Ablex.

Reading, Writing, and Retention of Under Represented Students: a University Responsibility

Dolores A. Escobar

Introduction

During the last few years, the media have highlighted education in unparalleled fashion. There have been numerous television documentaries on effective schools, problem schools, honor students, and dropouts. Radio and TV talk shows abound with commentaries and opinions about school. Almost monthly another national or state commission publishes a report on the status of schools, students, and teachers in the United States.

Demands for reform at all levels of schooling have come from many segments of the profession and population at large. While commission findings may emphasize different areas of reform, two themes consistently recur. The first refers to students' lack of basic skills in reading, composition, and mathematics. While earlier commissions decried students' lack of these rudimentary skills, recent reports recognize gains in the "back-to-basics" movement of the 1970s and 1980s but lament the stress on the mechanics of writing and mathematics rather than the ability to analyze, extend ideas, and reason. They would have schools stress higher levels of literacy and thinking.

The second recurring theme refers to the changing demographics of urban areas in the United States and the need for improvement in the education of "at risk" students who often are from minority racial, ethnic, and linguistic backgrounds, and/or from low socio-economic levels. Commissions and blue ribbon committees urge the formation of *effective* educational programs to stem the dropout rates and to provide adequate training for the future work force of the nation.

Demographic trends in Southern California indicate that the school population is rapidly becoming non-white (Latino and Asian) and limited English speaking. This poses one of the greatest challenges for educators from preschool to the university. How one university is attempting to meet the challenge of developing student literacy, particularly composition skills, will be discussed. The development of the "remedial program," the characteristics of the students, the effectiveness of the program, recent trends, and some of the philosophic considerations of a university involved in remediation will comprise the discussion.

The beginning of a remedial program

Recognition of the changing nature of students entering four-year institutions, particularly their academic deficiencies, became apparent at California State University, Northridge, in the early 1970s. The change signaled a trend throughout the CSU System which occurred following the social upheavals of the 1960s. During this time, minority groups demanded educational equity; their demands, along with a national awareness of social inequities, resulted in the growth of federally supported educational programs such as the Educational Opportunity Program (EOP), as well as the expansion of the "special admissions" category which brought to the university larger numbers of students who were not traditionally prepared.

To some in academia the change in the student population signified disaster, a disintegration of academic standards. To others it signified an enrichment of the college community through the infusion of cultural and linguistic variety into what had been a largely white, middle class campus in the northern end of the San Fernando Valley.

Moreover, by the middle 1970s, it became clear that the culturally and racially different students were not the only students who were unprepared. There had been a general decline in SAT scores, and substantial numbers of students who met minimum admission requirements were unable to succeed in college-level mathematics and language courses. Nevertheless, the concept of remediation was slow to develop within the university community. It became a somewhat unpopular concept in a hostile environment.

By 1975 the chancellor of the California State Universities and Colleges, Glen Dumke, established a systemwide task force on writing. Its recommendations were eventually adopted by the board of trustees and formed the basis upon which remediation programs were established:

1. The board endorsed the concept of a systemwide writing proficiency/diagnostic examination for entering lower division students. An English Placement Test (EPT) was initiated in the fall of 1977 on the CSUN campus.

2. The board recommended to the chancellor that remediation programs directed to the improvement of student writing skills be authorized when appropriate, with workload credit permitted for faculty. Although graduation credit for students need not be granted.

3. The board endorsed the principle that all students entering the CSUC after the implementation date of the proficiency diagnostic examination be required to demonstrate their competency with regard to writing skills as a requirement for graduation. A Writing Proficiency Examination (W.P.E.) was administered in spring 1977 at CSUN. (1)

In 1980, Chancellor Dumke issued Executive Order 338 that directed all campuses in the system to address the issue of "Entry Level Learning Skills" and to establish a program for remediation. By 1982 all campuses were to:

1. Determine the appropriate level of skills for English language and mathematical computation.

2. Institute means for determining whether new students possessed such skills.

3. Identify those courses and other means for achieving requisite skill levels where they do not exist.

4. Institute policies and procedures to insure that baccalaureate credit is not granted for such courses. (2)

As with most programs imposed from above, the remedial program struggled to evolve as an integral part of the university. It took various forms on different campuses, and it suffered from the incredibly slow and complicated curriculum development processes typical of most university campuses.

A remedial program takes form

Chancellor Dumke's executive order was implemented on each campus within the framework of local constraints, tradition, and politics. For example, at CSUN in the late 1960s, two ethnic studies departments had been established, Chicano Studies and Pan-African Studies. Each had its curriculum and its clientele, many of whom fell in the "at-risk" category. However, traditionally it was the Department of English that provided instruction in composition. Furthermore, historically the School of Education provided students with help in reading through its university reading laboratory. Nevertheless, funds from the Chancellor's Office became available to establish a Learning Resource Center to provide assistance to students in all academic areas. There was also an established faculty committee structure which governed curriculum and program development. The realities of existing conditions and structures called for meetings and compromises which resulted in a unique set of policies and programs.

At CSUN three parallel remedial composition programs evolved — one housed in the English Department, one in the Pan-African Studies Department, and one in the Chicano Studies Department. Although each department offered developmental courses in writing, there has been a concerted effort to coordinate and standardize the curriculum. The instructors have met regularly to develop relatively common syllabi and common examinations with which to assess students. The three departments have worked as a team to administer and score the University English Placement Test and the Writing Proficiency Examination.

The remedial mathematics courses have been offered within the Mathematics Department. The remedial reading course for teacher candidates who do not pass the screening tests for admission to the program has been offered in the Secondary Education Department.

The University Reading Clinic and the Learning Resource Center have developed as somewhat separate entities. The Reading Clinic has been an individually oriented facility where any student can go for diagnosis of reading difficulties and receive a prescription for remediation. The student works through the prescribed program on his/her own schedule. The Learning Resource Center has offered much the same service to students in all academic skill areas. It has provided tutoring services for specific courses such as Business Calculus, as well as provided workshops designed to develop such specific competencies as might be needed to pass a California Basic Education Skills Test (CBEST). All staffing and instructional support for these facilities now have become the responsibility of the campus, with little or no outside supplementary funds.

Characteristics of remedial students and results of the program at CSUN

In the early 1980s it became clear that our entering student population would need remedial services for some time to come. The programs initiated would not be short lived or terminate in five years as some had anticipated. They would not be stop-gap measures until the secondary schools shored up their programs and sent us fully prepared students. Therefore, in 1983 the provost at CSUN established a Committee on Remedial Education to analyze student need and to consider the university's responsibility to meet those needs.

First, the committee looked back over the previous five years to determine the characteristics of the students and patterns of progress: Who were the students? What was their primary language? What was their ethnic background and citizenship status? What were their intended majors?

The committee also was expected to predict the future need based upon demographic trends in order to guide programmatic development with sensitivity to university resource expectations. To what extent would the remedial program drain resources from the "traditional" programs of the university? These and related questions were of considerable interest. They formed the basis of continued discussion and debate within the Academic Senate and among school deans. Equally important, future development of the remedial program was to be considered in terms of program results which could be assessed by student retention and success in subsequent studies.

An analysis of the program from its implementation in 1977 through spring 1984 produced interesting data:

— Almost 50 percent of the Educational Opportunity students could not move directly into college-level courses. Forty-eight percent enrolled in both the developmental writing and developmental mathematics courses.

— Hispanic students tended to enroll in developmental courses in the Chicano Studies Department; Blacks enrolled in the Pan-African Studies Department; Asians and Whites enrolled in the English Department courses.

— Of the 600 international students enrolled at CSUN in 1983, only 5 percent enrolled in developmental courses.

— Between 1977 and 1984, 20,000 students had taken the English Placement Test, and the percentages of students failing to make minimum scores increased from 34 percent in 1977 to 55 percent in 1983. (3)

— Recent test scores indicate comparable figures, with the average number of students falling below the minimum EPT score in 1985 and 1986 amounting to 43 percent.

These figures should be considered in the light of several factors. For example, a large increase in the percentage of failures in the English Placement Test coincided with an influx of resident aliens of Asian descent who tested very high in mathematics but low in English skills. Furthermore, perfecting the nature of the examination and the process of scoring it, as well as the increased sophistication of the graders, may have affected the outcomes.

The success of the program has been demonstrated clearly through subsequent student achievement in freshman level composition courses in the fall and spring semesters of 1983.

TABLE I

Student Achievement in Freshman Composition

Remedial Courses	Freshman Courses	Percent Passing
Chicano Studies	Chicano Studies English Pan-African Studies	69.9
English	ChS Eng PAS	80.1
Pan-African Studies	ChS Eng PAS	69.45
		(4)

The question of program effectiveness has been studied on a number of CSU campuses. One study recently completed at CSU Fresno of 1488 freshmen is of particular interest. It focused on the English Placement Tests subscores and their use in assigning freshmen to beginning English courses. The study has provided some insights about the test's relationship to future academic success, the relationships between reading, composition, and academic achievement, as well as such factors as ethnicity and English-as-a-Second-Language (ESL) status, which could affect student retention.

Basically, the study underscored the interrelatedness between composition and reading. The authors recommended that universities develop reading improvement programs in as thorough a manner as they had writing programs. The study cautioned against using the English Placement Test score or any standardized test score as the sole means for student placement. It also raised serious questions about the university's lack of concern for ethnic, racial, and cultural differences in everything from test anxiety and test-taking ability to culture bound test items. The study also brought out socio-cultural factors, such as group identification and support, as being positive for retention of minority students.

The study verified the use of specific course grades, particularly English composition course grades, as reliable predictors of future academic success, especially if such courses emphasized the development of competencies needed in future university work. Of all the sub-scores of the English Placement Test, the essay portion proved to be most predictive of academic success. The study also pointed out that reliance on test scores alone overlooked the special gifts or abilities that students from varied backgrounds brought to the university. (5) (This is particularly pertinent to the English-as-a-Second-Language (ESL) students who comprise a substantial number of those in remedial classes).

Finally, the Fresno study, to some extent, supported several practices at CSUN: 1) the use of course work in preparation for freshman composition; 2) the use of ethnic studies departments to provide role models and support services for non-minority as well as minority students; 3) the institutionalization of the program which has resulted in a University-supported Writing Program Coordinator, as well as other faculty and staff to direct portions of the program and assess its effectiveness.

*Current trends within the university's remedial
program*

An indication of the extent of the writing program's
institutionalization can be seen in acceptance of the
concept that improvement of student writing is an all-
university function. This semester a new project is being
implemented, entitled "Writing Across the Disciplines."
It can be summarized as follows:

Its Goal: To improve student writing in upper division
courses across all disciplines by developing
appropriate assignments and examination methods.

Its Method: Four English faculty members will receive
released time (12 units) in the spring term to provide
intensive training in writing to 30 faculty members
from various disciplines. The training will include,
but is not limited to, the following: development of
effective writing assignments and essay
examinations, examination of methods of evaluating
student writing, application of formal and informal
writing to increase student comprehension of reading
assignments. The training will provide faculty with a
set of appropriate student assignments, writing
projects, and evaluation techniques for student
writing.

The Timetable: Interim Session — Two half-day
workshops for 30 faculty members from various
disciplines.

Spring Term — The 30 faculty members will be
divided into four groups. Each group will have one of
the participating English faculty assigned to it as
workshop leader. The workshop leader will direct a
series of seminars for the group in which faculty will
produce assignments, discipline-based writing
samples, and methods of evaluating student writing.

Thirty faculty members will meet with the four
English faculty workshop leaders to share solutions to
common writing problems in their disciplines.

Workshop leaders will hold a series of one-on-one
conferences with faculty members of their respective
groups.

Workshop activities will include bringing outside
experts in writing to the campus for the 30 faculty
members. (6)

This kind of project is most consistent with current thinking on the development of writing skills as a part of critical thinking in content areas. It is designed to provide students with opportunities to use writing to organize thoughts, make inferences, and synthesize information that has meaning for them. Equally important, the project is designed to sensitize faculty in all disciplines to the fact that they are to some extent teachers of reading and composition.

A related campus trend is the revision of a substantial number of courses in the social sciences, sciences, and humanities to include "writing components." Syllabi now contain writing assignments which will be graded for composition quality as well as content. The number of students admitted to these courses is limited to 35, a substantial reduction in class size. However, in order to teach such a course, the professor must agree to attend a workshop on the teaching of writing. Over 50 courses have been revised and reclassified this year.

Because the challenge does not appear to be diminishing, every avenue is being explored to help improve student literacy. Computer assisted instruction is being utilized in college-level English composition courses and, when appropriate, in the remedial courses.

To date, attempts at CSUN to document the effectiveness of computer assisted instruction in composition have been inconclusive. One of the most complete studies was initiated in 1985 by a member of the English Department under the auspices of an Instructional Improvement Grant. He used a software program, HOMER, developed by Michael E. Cohen at UCLA, to assist in the teaching of composition revision. The program was designed to help students revise compositions independently. Essentially, the program attacked "school style" and "official style" composition, i.e., extensive use of "to be" and passive voice. It also evaluated writing for excessively long sentences and monotonous prose.

The evaluation of the project indicated that students could use the program effectively. By mid-semester all students in the experimental group were able to cope with the technology, whether they had previous experience with computers or not. However, the HOMER program did not save instructor time, nor did it replace the instructor as the primary resource. The students still needed close guidance to overcome writing problems that were not recognized by the program. However, the students did consider the program helpful, and 92 percent stated that they would recommend the class to a friend. (7)

Extending the university's responsibility for remedial education

Has the university's role in remedial education been extended purely as a matter of necessity or expediency? Certainly, the prediction in 1977 that in five years remedial programs at the university would "self-destruct" have proven false. Today no one is entertaining thoughts about an exact duration for such programs, especially in the face of demographic projections which indicate that in California by the year 2000 the Latino population will increase by 52 percent and the Asian population by 69 percent. These two groups will comprise 27 percent and 12 percent, respectively, of the state's population. (8) Ethnic, racial, and linguistic minorities are already the majority of the student population in many urban school districts in California.

Actually, there has been increased participation by university personnel in programs to improve literacy at all levels of schooling. This participation may be considered attempts to eliminate the need for remedial education at the university level, but that simplistic rationale has to give way to the idea that there is genuine interest in understanding such areas as how individuals best develop literacy, how language use is related to cognitive development, how a second language is acquired most efficiently, or how language competency is related to issues involving educational equity and social mobility. It is clear from the literature of research in the field that language development is a complex, long-term process that must begin in the early grades and continue throughout the student's schooling.

Evaluations of existing instructional practice, such as conducted by the California Assessment Program, point out that teachers must consciously strive to teach to the highest levels of language competency through specific instruction in analysis of literature, exercises in inference, and practice in creative composition. How these techniques can best be implemented is of interest to the academician as well as the high school or elementary classroom teacher. To find answers to these important questions, partnerships and cooperative investigations involving the university faculty and teachers in the field have been established.

Two of the most ambitious programs underway at CSUN involve participation in the California Writing Project and the California Academic Partnership Program. Both are aimed at improving the language instruction of upper elementary, junior, and senior high school students through continued, professional development of teachers. Both demand considerable involvement of English and Education professors in public school classrooms. This involvement, in turn, has resulted in improved course content and methods of instruction in university classrooms.

The California Academic Partnership Program has been designed to help teachers guide learning from text, in order to develop critical thinking skills and to apply those skills in composition.

The California Writing Project has provided a professional development model which utilizes a writing workshop technique conducted by classroom teachers who have gone through an intensive program of training in methods of teaching composition. Both of these programs target the high school as the place to eliminate the need for remedial education at the university.

However, each year the list of outreach programs to recruit minority students has grown. A number of these, such as the Future Scholars Program and the College Readiness Program, have been designed to assist in preparing these students to gain admission to the university. This effort has been made with the full understanding that these students will need special programs in their lower division work if they are to be retained through to graduation.

Furthermore, every school within the university has been urged to develop and implement its own recruitment program in an effort to correct the underrepresentation of minority students. For example, while Latinos in Los Angeles and Ventura Counties comprise as high as 43 percent of the students in kindergarten through twelfth grade, they make up only 15 percent of the high school graduates and 8 percent of the CSUN student body. (9) This disparity has been addressed in a report initiated by the Commission on Hispanic Underrepresentation and published by the CSU Chancellor's Office, *Hispanics and Higher Education: A CSU Imperative,* 1984, which recommends increased attention to the problem, including financial support.

Though some faculty in the State University System may be awaiting the day of rescue from teaching basic skills so that they may teach "real" college courses, the reality of our community does not indicate immediate relief from the need for remedial programs. However, does this outlook toward the future necessarily mean a lessening of academic rigor? What are academicians learning as they become involved with elementary and secondary schools? What improvements are classroom teachers implementing as a result of increased interaction with university personnel and participation in professional development programs?

Most important, what is the mission of the State University if it is not to educate the people within its community? Finally, what talents do the students who have survived the system bring to the university? What can we learn from them, and how can we develop their talents so as to enable them to be contributing members of an increasingly demanding society?

REFERENCES

1 G. Larson. *Report on Remediation at CSUN*. Academic Affairs Planning Council, 1985, p. 5.

2 Ibid. p. 4.

3 Ibid. p. 11, p. 12.

4 Ibid. Appendix A, Tables VI through XI.

5 L. Aycock, et al. *A Study of English Placement Test Subscores and Their Use in Assigning CSU Fresno Freshmen to Beginning English Courses*. E.P.T. Test Development Committee, 1986 (monograph).

6 R. Lid. "Writing Across the Disciplines." A Proposal for the use of Discretionary Funds, CSUN, 1986.

7 J. Clendenning. *Using HOMER: An Experiment in Computer Assisted Instruction for Composition*. Report to the Research and Grants Committee, CSUN, 1984.

8 Catherine Minicucci and Mario Muniz. Presentation at the Educational Equity Conference, CSUN, California State Department of Education.

9 Ibid.

10 T. Arciniega. *Hispanics and Higher Education: A CSU Imperative, Part I*. Report of the Commission on Hispanic Underrepresentation, Office of the Chancellor, CSU, 1984, pp. 17-18.

Cultural and Linguistic Consideration in Developing the Composition Skills of Chicano Students

Juan M. Flores

Research literature in language development supports the important role of the primary language and culture in developing second language skills for language minority students (Cummins, 1981). This essay addresses the cultural and linguistic considerations that may affect the development of writing skills in Chicano students.

Composition and language proficiency

Teachers often distinguish between Chicano and Mexican students according to their verbal fluency in English. If the student speaks English fluently and easily without any obvious or interfering accents, he is likely to be categorized as Chicano or Mexican-American (English only) and will be expected to function in English as a native. On the other hand, if this student appears limited in English proficiency, then he may be placed in bilingual instruction, if indeed such instruction is available at his school site.

Many students are classified as fluent in English without considering their full range of English proficiencies and skills. That is, teachers most likely sample a student's oral proficiency and, on this basis, decide on a student's English proficiency.

Most Chicano and Mexican students display linguistic skills in English along a continuum extending from basic communication skills to deeper, more academic skills. For the purposes of this paper, I will use the term Chicano to refer to both Mexican and Chicano students and to characterize their range of linguistic proficiency.

Teachers often pay the most attention to those most superficial, basic, interpersonal communication skills (Cummins, 1981), when making placement decisions, thus assuming that these students are more proficient in English than they truly are. These students typically have lost most of the obvious characteristics of one who is learning English (accent, halting speech) but have not acquired the cognitive and academic linguistic proficiencies that represent the skills of academic success.

As the number of limited English-proficient students continues to grow, increasingly, more students will be making the transition to verbal English fluency. In addition, the peer pressure to learn to speak English as soon as possible and the job realities requiring English skills will hasten the development of these basic interpersonal communication skills.

Cummins says that an inadequate understanding of what is meant by "English proficiency" is likely to result in the creation of academic deficits in the language of minority students (1981, p. 4). Often students are identified as fluent English proficient based on their ability to use the surface features of the language. Indeed, one can expect that these students will be able to handle the surface features of the English language within two years of exposure to English. Are these students proficient in English? Probably not. Quite often, our assessment of their proficiency to function verbally in English is enough for us to place these students in an English curriculum. Then we are chagrined because of the apparent discrepancies between their often low verbal scores and their more normal nonverbal scores. We often dismiss the ESL, (English-as-a-second language) possibility, accepting that the student has not progressed at a normal rate, and thus setting lower academic expectations for them (Cummins, 1981).

We realize now that language proficiency consists of surface features representing basic interpersonal communication skills (BICS), as well as the underlying features which consist of cognitive and academic linguistic proficiencies (CALP), the underlying proficiencies of a language that allow us to move beyond surface communication and into the realm of investigation, concept formation, and critical thinking.

We have also accepted the common underlying proficiency of language: that concept formation and critical thinking skills are developed and shared across languages and that strong skills transfer. The cognitive and academic skills and abilities that students possess in Spanish can help them significantly in eventually developing English skills.

Composition and culture

However, the sociocultural determinants of minority students' school failure often are more fundamental than the linguistic factors (Cummins, 1981). Often acculturation, or lack thereof, is pointed to as the reason why Chicano students experience school failure. Educators have often assumed that the more ethnically and culturally unacculturated a student is, the more likely he is to experience failure in school. Interestingly, the opposite perspective seems to be developing in the research literature internationally (Chesarek, 1981; Bhatngar, 1980; Skutnabb-Kangas and Toukomaa, 1976, as cited in Cummins, 1981). According to this research, acculturated students tend to perform less well academically than students who continue to use their primary language and who maintain strong ties to their home culture.

The growing number of minority language students in our public schools makes these concerns and cautions all the more real. Most teachers will have at least one limited English-proficient student who will need some help in learning to express himself in writing and in accepting the validity of his experiences and cultural background. These teachers will be faced with the jobs of creating feelings in these students that their experiences and backgrounds are worth writing about and that their home language is an important and valued means of communicating. All of this points to a broader, more significant finding in the literature: when schools reinforce the minority language child's cultural identity, promote the development of the child's primary language, and make instruction in English meaningful to the child's previous experience, then minority language students experience academic success and develop high English literacy skills (Cummins. 1981).

The Foxfire experience: an effective writing program

One of the most important recommendations that surfaces from the research literature is that effective writing programs will develop students who "believe that what they have to say is important (and) are motivated to write, because they feel that they have something important to say." (California State . . . 1983)

Giving validity to the experience of students is important enough in any English composition class, but it becomes especially critical in classrooms with students who come from culturally and linguistically different backgrounds. These are the students who quite often feel that they have the least to say in the traditional classroom (Wiggington, 1975).

The Foxfire project rose out of the concerns of Eliot Wiggington, a high school teacher who was frustrated at the lack of success he was having in teaching English literature and composition to his poor, white Appalachian-background students in Rabun Gap, Georgia. Wiggington realized that he needed to put aside the traditional tools of English composition in order to help his students succeed in school. He chose to work toward improving their self concept by helping them feel proud of their culture.

Wiggington began by validating the culture of the Appalachian hill people and instilling in his students the desire to want to learn more about their rich backgrounds. His students ultimately developed and produced Foxfire, a magazine that was devoted to investigating and showcasing the lore of the Appalachian hill people.

Wiggington's students came into contact with "special people" in the community who had some unique gift or talent related to their culture. These people were the elders who had the ghost stories, folk remedies, skills in craft and building, and other talents. The students produced articles on topics ranging from faith healing to moonshining. Through this educational experience they were able to develop an appreciation for their parents and their culture that they most likely did not previously have.

Foxfire and the barrio folklore

Many Chicano children arrive at school already possessing a rich folklore that was passed on to them by their parents. Before they were old enough to enter kindergarten, they could recite poems, sayings, and songs that their parents had once also recited as children.

However, through their educational experiences, some of these children implicitly learn that the only things worthy of learning are facts found in books or passed on by their teachers. These covert and sometimes overt lessons have often had the effect of invalidating the cultural experiences of the children and leaving these developing writers with the feeling that their reality did not have a legitimate place in the classroom.

The teacher who hopes to develop the writing skills of Chicano students has tremendous resources in the homes and neighborhoods of their students that can make important contributions to the development of the budding Chicano writer. Every barrio has its history and lore, and if we can guide our students in the study of their community closely enough, they can find a valuable store of historical and cultural richness.

Recently a teacher in Madera, California, developed an innovative project that involved the students in writing biographies of pioneers of the San Joaquin Valley. These children began with the journal of a pioneer to this valley and retraced his experiences as he journeyed with his family and companions to their destination. Through this process the children learned a great deal about the history and sociology of pioneers and, in the process, improved in their writing ability. This teacher was very successful in applying the methods of Eliot Wiggington to his classroom situation to motivate the students to write.

The history of California is full of the exploits and contributions of Chicanos, the investigation of which can serve to provide rich writing opportunities for students. Tomas Atencio calls this valuable store of historical and cultural richness "el oro del barrio," the gold and richness within our communities (1971).

Chicano children can benefit significantly when their lives and culture become an integral, important, and respected part of their experiences in school. Suddenly school becomes a reflection of them, and they begin to feel more of an integral part of it.

I was once involved in teaching a weekend enrichment class for gifted and talented migrant Chicano high school students. In the time we spent together in my class, the students produced a book of writings, poetry, sayings, and personal accounts, written in both Spanish and English, that have remained with them over the years. Indeed, many years after the class, I have seen copies of their book in the possession of former students. For many of them, it had been their first successful experience in a composition class. They felt confident in the purpose of the class and worked intently on assignments that involved things of importance to them.

Many creative and talented teachers who work with Chicano students have developed and applied a Foxfire "Barrio Folklore" approach to the teaching of composition and have helped students produce books and magazines describing the experiences their students brought with them to the classroom. Articles are beginning to appear in the professional literature describing these novel efforts in composition that serve to encourage Chicano children to write on the basis of their background and experiences. Recently, Dueñas published an article describing her experiences in teaching composition to Chicano students at the college level (1982).

The students of these innovative teachers have demonstrated improved writing skills as a result. In addition, they have been assisted by these insightful teachers to discover, understand, and accept their own families, their cultural heritage, and the richness of their communities. They have benefited doubly.

REFERENCES

Atencio, Tomas. El Cuaderno (de vez en cuando), Dixon, New Mexico: Academia de la Nueva Raza, 1971.

Cummins, James. "The Role of the Primary Language in the Learning of Language Minority Students," in Schooling and Language Minority Students: A Theoretical Framework, California State Department of Education, 1981.

Brazee, P.E., and J.V. Kristo. "Creating a Whole Language Classroom with Future Teachers," Reading Teacher, 39:422-8, January 1986.

Duenas, Roseanne. "Teaching Mexican American Students to Write: Capitalizing on the Culture," English Journal, November 1982.

Handbook for Planning an Effective Writing Program: Kindergarten through Grade Twelve, Sacramento: California State Department of Education, 1984.

Wiggington, Eliot. Moments: The Foxfire Experience, Rabun Gap, Georgia: The Foxfire Foundation, 1975.

"Developing Social Studies and Laguage Arts Skills Using Community Resources," Social Education, 47(7):536-39, November-December 1983.

"Language Arts in Multicultural Education" (Symposium), Language Arts, 63:442-71, 1986.

"The Forms, Functions and Values of Literacy: Reading for Survival in a Barrio as a Student," NABE: The Journal of the National Association of Bilingual Education, 1(7):21-39, Fall 1984.

Is This Just Another Swing of the Pendulum? That Depends...

Janet Kierstead

In the midst of a massive educational reform movement, skeptics point to the past and ask, "Is this just another swing of the pendulum?" Their question is well founded, and the answer depends on how well we understand where we've been, where we are now, and where we might be headed. Only by drawing upon a clear understanding of the past can we hope to make the decisions that will take us in the direction we want to go. But just what direction is that?

A vision of excellence within the California experience

National leaders call for a move from "back-to-basics" toward "excellence" in education, yet that term has not been well defined. So, while local practitioners agree on the need for change, they lack a vision of excellence to guide their planning. In California the state department of education is facilitating the process of defining that vision and helping educators translate it into classroom practice. I have been involved in this effort and describe it here as an example of what can be done.*

Under the leadership of Superintendent of Public Instruction Bill Honig, groups of practitioners from around the state have come together regularly over the

---

*The ideas expressed here have most recently become an integral part of training provided by the California State Department of Education's California School Leadership Academy. I wish to express my appreciation to Sally Mentor, Assistant Superintendent, Instructional Support Division, California State Department of Education, for her keen insights and leadership in these activities.

past several years to describe what they want for their students. Facilitated by state department of education staff, these various committees have created philosophy statements (Frameworks) and described standards (Model Curriculum Standards) in science, math, English/language arts, history/social science, foreign language, and fine arts.

Out of this effort a vision of excellence for California schools is emerging. In this vision, all students — regardless of incoming level of performance — have a common core curriculum which provides them with a sound academic background and promotes literacy in the various disciplines, which may also be integrated. For example, students may study literature, history/ social science, and language arts together. Further, recognizing that each new generation of students is developing a set of values within their own peer culture, the curriculum is designed to foster a strong sense of traditional values. For instance, as they gain knowledge of the past, students discuss how personalities in literature and history dealt with such issues as honesty, responsibility, respect for human diversity. As they consider what course of action is appropriate within a present day situation, students are encouraged to temper their decisions with reasoned moral and ethical judgments.

Drawing upon all they have learned, students carry out projects in which they apply their skills and concepts to "real life" situations. For example, a young student studying nutrition may survey his classmates to develop a list of their favorite foods, design a balanced menu from that list, and present it to the staff in the school cafeteria. An older student may select a contemporary topic of special interest, perhaps an environmental issue, research the factors surrounding it, and search for a parallel from the past which may shed some light on it. Having gathered that information, he conducts an opinion survey regarding a possible course of action, perhaps video taping his interviews. He then presents a report to the appropriate audience, using flow charts, timelines, video tapes, etc., to illustrate his findings and to explain his recommendations. Such projects serve as evidence that

students are developing the ability to act as culturally
literate adults, fully contributing members of society.

Since the vision initially was defined by a relatively
small group of practitioners, the state department has
now moved on to a necessary next step: sharing that
vision with the much larger group of local leaders and
decisionmakers and enlisting their help in refining and
promoting it. This is being done through workshops
throughout the state. These are not the usual "top-
down" information sessions. Instead, facilitators
"practice what they preach" by using strategies
envisioned for excellent classrooms. They involve
participants in large- and small-group, cooperative,
learning activities to read, analyze, and discuss articles
which explain the thinking behind the vision. They also
use individual and small-group problem-solving
strategies to devise examples of how that vision might
look when translated into classroom practice in each of
the subject areas. They create skits, murals, flow charts,
etc., to present their ideas to one another. During the
closing activity of the workshop, they help one another
devise plans to provide similar experiences for
practitioners and decisionmakers back home.

Most participants in these workshops enthusiastically
embrace the vision. Once they have clarified the basic
intent, they turn to the question of "how."
Administrators ask how to get teachers to do this, and
teachers ask how to get administrators to support them
so they *can* do it!

A lesson from the past

Setting aside the example of the California experience
for now, let's look at what we can learn from the past
about how to bring about change in education. We have
already been through several pendulum swings in
thinking and practice over this century. For instance,
we began with a swing from the established
"traditional" methods of lecture and group recitation to
"progressive education," with its emphasis on more
actively engaging students in learning (Dewey, 1916).
This was followed by a return to traditional practices.
Next came a swing to the more experiential "open

education" (Holt, 1967; Silberman, 1973). Then finally, we went "back to basics," a trend with an emphasis on academic standards and discipline (Ravich, 1983).

Typically, teachers react to changes in thinking in a variety of ways. Some misunderstand the ideas or cannot work them out. These teachers go too far, so in many classrooms progressive education became laissez-faire, open education became "do-your-own-thing," and "back-to-basics" became watered down content and drill and practice of skills in isolation. Others seem to be unaffected. They are unaware of, ignore, or resist the call for change. Or, perhaps they experiment with the new ideas for awhile and then slip back into the usual routine. Still others seem to be working toward a vision within themselves. They do not see themselves as using *either* traditional methods *or* an experiential approach but rather, are striving to strike a balance between the two. They take something from each new point of view and use it to expand what they are already doing. Over the years these teachers have created approaches which represent a synthesis of traditional and experiential methods, a balance between extreme swings of the pendulum. In other words, the third group of teachers is approaching or has already reached the vision of excellence guiding the current reform movement, and as I will explain, become one of our most valuable resources.

Looking back, it seems a critical lesson can be drawn from this: *we need to more clearly define the vision, we must see that it reaches the general population of teachers, and we must support them as they work to translate it into classroom practice.*

Again using the California experience as an example, the Frameworks and Model Curriculum Standards clearly define the vision, and local school districts are now using them as a tool for curriculum planning. At the same time, an encouraging thing is beginning to happen. That "third group" of teachers mentioned earlier is beginning to step forward to share with other teachers the classroom strategies they have developed. So, the vision is much more clearly defined now than in any of the earlier reform movements and is beginning to affect more and more classroom teachers. But this cannot be left to chance. More must be done to ensure widespread teacher involvement and to provide ongoing support for their efforts to change.

The present situation

In working with practitioners, I find that most of them currently stand in one of four fairly distinct positions in the movement from "back-to-basics" toward a middle ground between extremes. (1) Where they stand can be identified by their views regarding the purpose of schooling — whether they plan for relatively narrow or broad student outcomes — and by the classroom practice they employ. These four positions are outlined below. As you read through them, notice that they represent a process of expansion, that teachers moving through these positions over the years, as so many have done, have slowly been building upon previous practice to create a broader, richer experience for students.

Four positions in the movement from back-to-basics

The First Position. Here the teacher focuses on what students are to *know* and uses a test of information at the end of the course to assess learning. The course consists of a series of lessons, usually following a textbook: the teacher lectures and gives demonstrations, the students take a quiz, the teacher gives more input, another quiz, etc. After several lessons, students take an end-of-chapter test. This sequence is repeated until the course ends with the final test.

The Second Position. Here the teacher focuses on what students are to *know,* what *basic skills* they are to acquire, and what *understanding* they are to develop. Behavioral objectives guide planning. The assessment at the end of the course is a test of information, including essay and abstract problems. The course unfolds like the first approach but with a bit more active student participation as input is followed with guided and independent practice.

The Third Position. In addition to *knowledge* and *understanding,* here the teacher expresses concern for developing the more affective student outcomes, such qualities as *independence, responsibility, creativity, enthusiasm, and a sense of values.* At the same time two changes begin to appear in the classroom.

— lessons are organized into units of study, each with a focus on a particular topic and ending with a culminating activity which applies and extends skills and concepts in a new situation. At the end of each unit, for instance, students demonstrate what they have learned by creating a mural, timeline, set of recommendations, skit, three-dimensional model, etc. (2)

— the teacher still gives directed lessons as in the second position, but also uses other instructional strategies, such as cooperative learning, synectics, inquiry.

In addition to the usual test, the teacher assesses learning by observing and questioning students as they carry out their projects at the end of each unit. In this position, each unit stands alone. While some may be related to others, it occurs more by chance than by design.

The Fourth Position. Here student outcomes are expanded to include what students are to *know, understand, and be able to do in the "real world."* Thus, a literacy statement — what a literate adult is able to do in the discipline — guides planning, and students are expected to carry out an end-of-year project to serve as evidence that they have reached the long-term goal. Rather than a series of unrelated elements, the units are connected: the culminating activity in one is designed to incorporate and extend skills and concepts developed during the culminating activity of the others. Thus, what students are expected to do at the end of each unit becomes increasingly complex, so that by the end of the year/course they are able to carry out a relatively sophisticated project.

Expanding into the fourth approach

Many teachers have slowly been moving through these positions over the years. While I am not certain that every teacher must go through these positions in sequence, I do find that using these positions as a framework for viewing classroom practice helps to see that we should value existing practice as a step in the right direction, as something upon which to build. This is critical, as too often individuals see reform movements as "either/or" questions. The framework makes it easier to view it as a process of expansion, a "yes/and-now-let's-add" situation.

Rather than urge teachers to leap too quickly into the fourth position, I find it more helpful to suggest the next step which will move them in that direction. The framework helps to see what the next step might be. For instance, a teacher in the first position who lectures skillfully is probably ready to incorporate guided and independent practice into that lecture format. But that teacher is probably not ready to try independent student projects, because that requires a much more complex system of management and organizational practices (Kierstead, 1986). Similarly, a teacher in the second position who feels comfortable allowing a measure of active student participation is probably ready to try incorporating one or two projects into a year's course of study. Experimenting with student projects will develop the management and organizational strategies needed to move on with confidence to the fourth position.

Once a teacher is able to give effective lessons and manage student projects, it is relatively easy to expand existing practice into the fourth approach. Following is an example of how to create a classroom curriculum plan by modifying an existing eighth grade history course.

1. Define Literacy in the Discipline. The first step is to define what the average citizen literate in history/ social science should be able to do. It might read as follows:

> A person literate in history/social science is able to apply the lessons from the past to a present situation, make recommendations tempered with reasoned moral and ethical judgments, and communicate them effectively to others.

2. Describe a Corresponding Final Project. The next step is to describe the *type* of project students might carry out to serve as evidence that they have reached the goal. This description is more specific than the literacy statements, yet allows students and teachers the latitude to design projects based on individual needs, strengths, and interests. It might state, for example, that the student should be able to carry out the following type of project:

— select a contemporary issue of special interest to the student;

— research events and arguments surrounding that issue;

— relate findings to a similar event in history;

— conduct opinion surveys regarding what should be done;

— write a report that describes the research, relates findings, and explains recommendations in light of moral and ethical considerations;

— present the report orally to the appropriate audience, using charts, diagrams, video tapes.

3. Determine Skills and Concepts Needed. The third step is to list what students must be able to do in order to carry out the project. In this example, they need to know how to conduct opinion surveys and carry out library research, give oral presentations, create visuals, and so forth.

4. Expand Existing Topics of Study To Include Culminating "Benchmark" Projects. Most teachers already follow a textbook or course outline, spending from two to six weeks developing a major topic. All they need to do here is pause at the end of each of these major topics and add a culminating activity, a project that will develop *a few* of the skills and concepts needed for the end-of-year project. At the end of the first major topic, students might conduct library research on the probable cause and effect of an event in history and write a brief written report. This takes them out of the textbook and gives them experience with finding, selecting, and interpreting trade books, journals, and newspapers.

At the end of the next major topic, they might research a contemporary issue similar to an event discussed in the textbook, write a brief report, and give it orally using flow charts, diagrams, timelines, etc. After studying the next major topic, they might research a contemporary issue, conduct opinion surveys, and present results using graphs, charts, video tape, etc. The course proceeds in this manner until students have developed the skills and concepts needed to carry out the final project.

The new history course expands on the original course in several ways. Instead of using only the textbook, students now also draw from primary source materials, including historical records, current newspapers and news magazines, and personal interviews. Instead of relying almost exclusively on teacher-centered lessons, the teacher also allows students to provide information for one another in small cooperative learning groups and to carry out independent research. In addition, instead of relying exclusively on paper-pencil tests, the teacher also assesses learning by observing and questioning students as they carry out their projects.

In the workshops for local leaders and decisionmakers mentioned earlier, participants experiment with this curriculum design process. Grouped according to subject areas of their choice, they create classroom curriculum plans, complete with a series of benchmark projects leading to a final, end-of-course project. They also present visual illustrations of their plan to the entire group. Having participants carry out a short-term project within the workshop setting allows the facilitator to model how a teacher manages students during project periods in the classroom. This experience gives participants strategies they can use to help teachers understand how to design and manage the more active curriculum envisioned in the reform movement.

Viewing the current reform movement as a process of expansion and having practitioners experience some of the techniques they will need to accomplish it is critical. It helps both teachers and administrators feel more comfortable about trying to change and helps them see how it can be done. Where, then, does all this leave us in the question of how to move forward?

Moving forward

The vision of what we want for our students is getting clearer and clearer. Now the challenge is to help teachers translate that vision into classroom practice. We can approach them at the personal and at the policy level. On a personal level, we must recognize that the classroom is an extremely complex situation and that any attempt to change it is a problem-solving process of trial and error. Like the tide coming in at the beach, it is two steps forward and one step back, two forward and one back . . . We must be there with moral support and practical help for teachers as they work through both trial and error.

At the policy level, we must make a commitment to more fully involve teachers and to give them the opportunity to help one another work toward common goals through long-term staff development. This means involving teachers at the *beginning* of a district's efforts to strengthen curriculum, as goals are being established, and later, *sustaining their involvement* through an ongoing, group problem-solving process.

This represents an important departure from what we usually do. Typically when a new idea comes along, the local school district forms a committee, perhaps with teacher representatives, and the committee works out solutions to the problem of how to reach whatever the intent of that reform effort happens to be. Then experts "train" teachers to use the strategies that others have decided will move toward the vision of which they, the teachers, are never fully aware. This leaves the district committee knowledgable and committed, but leaves most teachers relatively untouched. They return to their classroom, put committee recommendations on the shelf, shut the door, and continue to teach much as before. Those who do embrace the new ideas return to their classrooms with the best of intentions but with no follow-up to remind them and no support as they work out the changes, most of them eventually go back to business as usual.

We have failed to recognize that *it is engaging in the problem-solving process that is so valuable.* Only by defining the vision in operational terms and rolling up their sleeves to figure out how to translate it into classroom practice will teachers understand and "buy in" to the reform movement. All teachers must go through the process. Imposing answers to the problem instead of supporting teachers as they work out answers for themselves has created havoc within our educational system. As Dewey (1940, p. 67) has pointed out:

> The system which makes no great demands upon originality, upon the continuous expression of individuality, works automatically to put and to keep the more incompetent teachers in the school . . . the best minds are drawn to the places where they can work most effectively. The best minds are not especially likely to be drawn where there is danger that they may have to submit to conditions which no self-respecting intelligence likes to put up with, where their time and energy are likely to be so occupied with details of external conformity that they have no opportunity for free and full play of their own vigor.

We have thus reached the crucial implementation stage in the California experience but have not yet fully come to grips with it, because most local administrators are still hoping to use the traditional top-down training methods to quickly convey to the general population of teachers what they should do.

A basic structure for the group problem-solving process has already been field tested in California with secondary teachers (Mohlman, Kierstead, and Gunlack, 1982). It consists of a series of working sessions held three weeks apart, with peers exchanging classroom visits between sessions to share ideas and give moral support. Coupling that with the curriculum design process described earlier, facilitators can take teachers through a three-phase process similar to the example that follows.

Phase I. The purpose of the first phase is to help teachers develop a common vision and to begin to feel that they are valued members in a team effort. Thinking back to the design process for expanding an existing history course, it is during phase one that participants carry out the first two steps in that process. To accomplish this with middle-grade history/social science teachers, for instance, the facilitator uses cooperative learning techniques to engage them in a dialogue concerning the basic intent of the reform movement. Participants read and discuss articles and subject-specific materials and share their own expertise before writing literacy statements and describing final projects.

During the first phase teachers are outlining long-term goals for major segments of schooling. For example, middle-grade history teachers would establish a project for graduating eighth graders, primary teachers would describe one for exiting third graders, etc. These "performance expectations" are sent to the district for review, returned to them with suggestions for improvement, modified by the teachers, resubmitted to the district, and so forth. During the first round of this staff development program in a district, the teachers are actually helping to *establish* district level performance expectations for students. As subsequent groups submit their ideas, these are used to *modify* existing expectations.

Phase II. Once performance expectations are agreed upon for the major segments of schooling (third, sixth, eighth, and twelfth grades), the second phase of the process begins. The purpose here is for teachers to work together to establish the performance expectations for each course or grade level and then, individually but with feedback from the group, create individual classroom curriculum plans. Again referring to the example given for expanding the history course, teachers now help one another through all four steps of that process, creating a plan for their own course. At this point the group breaks into small groups by grade level or specific course. In a group of primary teachers, for example, kindergarten teachers describe the type of project their students will carry out at the end of the year, the first-grade teachers devise one for their students, etc. Then the entire group looks at what each grade level subgroup has devised to see if they fit together to help students develop the skills and concepts they need to carry out the project envisioned for the end of third grade. Once end-of-year/ course goals are agreed upon, individual teachers or teachers grouped by grade level or course devise plans for benchmark projects and units of study.

Phase III. With classroom curriculum plans outlined, the third or implementation phase of the process begins. As individual teachers begin to modify classroom practice, they need to come together at least every three weeks or so for "working sessions," to compare notes and help one another devise new management and organizational strategies and acquire new instructional techniques. They may ask for help from "experts" who specialize in time management, cooperative learning techniques, etc. They will also find it helpful here to visit one another's classrooms between sessions, to exchange ideas, and give each other feedback as they begin to try new things.

Keep in mind that having teachers experience the process is what is important. A district committee could more quickly write literacy statements and outline final products. They could write classroom curriculum plans, complete with benchmark products and units of study. But by engaging teachers in group curriculum planning and problem solving processes, they are more likely to commit wholeheartedly to the reform effort and begin to develop the support system needed to sustain it.

Conclusion

As I work with parents and educators in the reform movement, they often ask whether this is just another swing of the pendulum. They ask in a rather detached, challenging way, as if they see it as something done to them by an outside force, something out of their control. It is as if they are waiting for someone else to do something about it, which is disturbing, for too much depends on it. The vitality and strength of our nation is at risk. We cannot afford to sit around and wait for "someone else" to act. We have a relatively brief window in time to make the reform movement count. We have more information than ever before about what needs to be done and how to go about doing it. We have the attention and good will of business and community leaders and the somewhat wary support of society in general. We must recognize that it is within our control to make this movement count and that it all depends on us. The time has arrived, but it will pass. Each of us must act *now* on what we know.

REFERENCES

Dewey, J. *Democracy and Education.* New York: The Macmillan Co., 1916.

Dewey, J. *Education Today.* New York: G. P. Putnam's Sons, 1940.

Holt, J. *How Children Fail.* New York: Pitman, 1967.

Kierstead, J. "Outstanding Effective Classrooms." In *Claremont Reading Conference, Forty-Eighth Yearbook,* Malcolm Douglass (ed.). Claremont, Calif.: Center for Developmental Studies, Claremont Graduate School, 1984.

Kierstead, J. "Direct Instruction and Experiential Approaches: Are They Really Mutually Exclusive?" *Educational Leadership, 42,* (May 1985): 25-30.

Kierstead, J. "How Teachers Manage Individual and Small-Group Work in Active Classrooms." *Educational Leadership, 44,* (October 1986): 22-25.

Mohlman, G., Kierstead, J., and Gundlack, M. "A Research-Based Inservice Model for Secondary Teachers." *Educational Leadership,* (October; 1982): 16-19.

Ravitch, D. "The Educational Pendulum." *Psychology Today.* (October; 1986): 63-71.

Silberman, C. *The Open Classroom Reader.* New York: Random House, 1973.

NOTES

1. The positions outlined here represent a continuum from "back to basics" to the middle ground between extreme swings of the pendulum. Gradations of approaches used by the relatively few practitioners who stand between the middle and the extreme experiential position are not considered here. While it might be helpful to analyze their positions at some future date, I have focused on the traditional side of the pendulum swing, because that is where the vast majority of practitioners currently stand.

2. Units of study usually follow a similar pattern. Spanning a period of from two to six weeks, they begin with an introduction and a description of what students will be held accountable for at the end of the unit: what they are expected to know, understand, and be able to do. Next comes a series of "lessons," instructional sequences to develop the content of the unit and to introduce the skills students will need to carry out their projects. Some of these lessons may follow a traditional format, others will involve cooperative group learning, inquiry, discovery, and so forth. The input stage is followed by the culminating activity, the application and extension stage of the unit. This is the time when students will apply to a new situation what they have learned in this and previous units. The projects are followed by a summary of the unit and the unit usually ends with a written assessment, a test of facts, with essay questions and abstract problems included.

Preschool Language Interaction in China, Japan, and Taiwan

Dana Davidson, Joseph Tobin, David Wu

This report offers a glimpse of language interaction found in programs for four-year-old children in three cultures: China, Japan, and Taiwan. All three societies are experiencing change in their preschool programs as Western influences, pressures from parents and governments, and the perceived needs of the children change. Preschools both reflect and affect their communities. They provide an important interface between families and their larger culture. They represent a microcosm of what each country considers important enough to pass on to their next generation.

A look at preschool programs provides insight into how children develop their language systems. By viewing children in preschool settings, attention, speaking, reading, and writing patterns emerge which may be reflective of a much larger scope of cultural attitudes and expectations. As we make judgments about others' language interaction, we also reveal something important about ourselves, our values, and beliefs about educating and socializing young children.

Our methodology for this research was simple: we videotaped a full day in preschools considered representative of their community. We chose Kyoto, Japan; Kunming, China; and Taipei, Taiwan. All three cities are home for over a million people. All three programs are used by professional and working class people who view preschool as an important step into elementary school. We edited the tapes to 15 minutes to present a quick vignette of the day. Those brief segments were then shown to parents, teachers, administrators, and students of early childhood education; each group was asked to rate the tapes of the three cultures' preschools, to make comments, and to fill out a values questionnaire on early childhood education.

Let us now consider the language systems and preschool language interaction patterns which emerge in China, Japan, and Taiwan.

CHINA is a country with over 300 million children (Zhang, 1982). With a formidable Single Child Policy currently in effect, each family seeks assurance that their only child will be well cared for in school. Over 60 percent of eligible Chinese children attend preschool. An interesting development in China is that of the Boarding School for very young children. Currently around 20 percent of the children living in large cities board at their preschool for six days per week and are home only from Saturday afternoon until Monday morning. The reasons for this are complex, including the need for the Communist Party to socialize hundreds of thousands of potentially spoiled single children. The teacher-pupil ratio for a class of four-year-old children in China is similar to that of the United States: one teacher for 16 children. A visitor to a class such as the one we taped may be surprised by the lack of electricity, running water, and learning materials. Beijing and some other cities are attempting to "develop" preschools to be more like ours. Yet, throughout China, conditions remain very different from what would be allowed in the United States.

There are hundreds of dialects in China. Mandarin Chinese is the official dialect of most higher education. Mandarin is over 4,000 years old. Most adults know at least 1200 Mandarin characters; the best dictionary of Mandarin Chinese has 40,000. Writing is ideographic with a pictorial basis.

Different Chinese dialects have differing tonal systems for speech. Mandarin has four tones; Cantonese has nine to twelve; Fukien (spoken in Taiwan) has seven to nine tones. The use of tones can make all the difference in the meaning of a word. The word "ma," for example, means four different things in Mandarin depending on the tonal pronunciation: "mother," "marijuana," "horse," and "to scold."

Attention is paramount in Chinese preschools. The role of rhyme, rote, and recitation becomes important (Rosenbaum, 1983). The emphasis on language learning in China is on enunciation, diction, memorization, and poise in speaking. Visitors are invariably impressed by the language command and self-possession of Chinese children who recite long stories and sing complicated songs.

Chinese adults tend to be impatient with mispronounced words or ill-formed characters. Pencils and paper or chalk and slates are used for early writing practice. Some pre-reading activities are taken from western intelligence tests. Our tape shows, for example, children copying a pattern for parquetry blocks, an item found on several individual IQ tests.

Few books are available to children to work with on their own. Most early reading and writing activities are didactic, teacher-led, and found at school rather than at home. There is little talking except when required and little free play. Children generally do not have free access to reading and writing materials.

JAPAN is a country currently very much in the news because of the high success rate of its educational system (Stevenson, 1985). Over 95 percent of Japanese four-year-olds attend preschool. Surprisingly, the Japanese early childhood curriculum does not emphasize much reading or writing. As most six-year-olds enter elementary school already reading, it is evident that most Japanese children begin to learn to read and write at home. Japanese, like Chinese, is also a language which requires a lifetime to learn (Stevenson et al., 1986).

Basically, there are three major Japanese systems for writing: 1) Kanji, which is based on Chinese characters. People who speak Japanese and not Chinese can communicate on a limited basis in Kanji although the grammatical systems are very different. Each Kanji character can be read with at least two different pronunciations; the correct pronunciation depends on the context. Kana is the phonetic writing system. It has many homonyms and the meanings can become obscure. For example, there are 10 words pronounced "dō," each with different meanings. "Hana" can mean nose or flower.

2) Hirigana is standard Kana for writing Japanese words. It is a syllabic system which makes use of 46 different syllables used in various combinations.

3) Katagana is a standard set of Japanese symbols used for adapting difficult-to-pronounce foreign words borrowed from other languages. For example, "jetto" means jet. Katagana has the same 46 Japanese sounds as Hirigana, but they are written in different symbols.

In addition to these three systems, most Japanese children begin to learn English before they are four. Many Japanese words and numbers are also "romanized" (in Japanese, called "romagi"). Japanese children, therefore, begin to learn four systems of reading and writing before they are six! By the first grade, most Japanese children know about 50 Kanji characters in addition to Hirigana, Katagana, and the ABCs. As in the United States, children in Japan usually learn familiar words first.

Japanese adults are fairly accepting of childish errors in pronunciation and writing. Children are often rewarded for simply trying to read or write; in our tape, for example, the teacher stamped smiling faces into the four-year-olds' workbooks without checking them at all for accuracy. Early reading is not an issue.

TAIWAN used to be called "Formosa" which is Portuguese for "beautiful island." Families in Taiwan have, over the centuries, been exposed to Portuguese and other European, Japanese, and Chinese influences. There are many ways in which Taiwan maintains its uniqueness, and Fukien, the language of Taiwan, is one. Families are more affluent in Taiwan than in China; Western, including American, influences over the economy are evident: children seem to have more freedom to move and speak freely. In the preschools there is variety and choice in the curriculum. Children speak noisily and frequently compared to China. Old Confucian ideals are evident, yet modified in Taiwan.

While the language used in Taiwan is also Mandarin Chinese, many people in Taiwan speak a form of "pidgin" or creole Mandarin called Fukien. There are seven to nine tones in Fukien instead of the four found in pure Mandarin, and these tones are not as strongly pronounced. There are more consonants in Fukien. There are slight variations in the writing of Fukien characters as well. Over the last 50 years, both the Taiwanese and especially the communist Chinese have simplified their characters in order to assure more people's ability to master and use the language. Literacy is higher in Taiwan than on the mainland of China.

The traditional Chinese emphasis on academic learning is higher in Taiwan, which experienced no cultural revolution. Many children face entrance exams into private elementary schools in Taipei and throughout Taiwan. By the age of five, most Taiwanese children can write around 100 characters; the average adult knows more than 1200. Early reading and writing are expected.

Language patterns in China, Japan, and Taiwan differ. Attending and production patterns are critical concerns, as concentration and "paying attention" are essential to learning the nuances of the three spoken languages of Mandarin, Japanese, and Fukien. Auditory discrimination, rhythmicity, respiration patterns, laryngeal tone, resonance, and intonation are especially important factors in the speaking of Mandarin and Fukien. Memory is crucial to the learning of all three languages, and rote and recitation are used to aid memory.

Semiotic functions, deferred imitation and mental imagery, and the universal need to use symbols to represent our world (Dleland, 1982) are evident in the reading and writing systems of all three languages. The sequence of learning based on personal experiences and interactions with adults and others appears to be transcultural, yet the features of the writing systems in

China, Japan, and Taiwan require somewhat variable strategies for mastery.

Meanings of both Chinese and Japanese are often abstract, and all three languages rely heavily on nuance. Much is left to the reader to understand on his/her own. In Japan, if a language misunderstanding occurs, problems are more often attributed to the listener than, as in English, the speaker. In all three cultures, a burden seems to be placed on individuals to be able to comprehend not only what is written or said, but also what is unwritten and unsaid. The attending behaviors encouraged in all three societies are probably very important to the comprehension of the many subtle aspects of Mandarin, Japanese, and Fukien.

Children learning to read must learn to recognize pictoriality or non-pictoriality, linearity, repetition of symbols, and familiarity. As Mandarin and Fukien are ideographic, the pictoriality factor becomes important for children to master (in English, our children seek symbols which do not look like pictures). Chinese and Taiwanese writing is independent of spoken words and represent ideas which are conveyed by speech. Oracy and literacy seem to be almost two separate systems to be developed by children.

Readers of Mandarin, Japanese, or Fukien usually develop a sense of linearity which proceeds from the top down and from right to left (English is, of course, left to right). Sometimes, however, Chinese or Japanese will be written from left to right; flexibility, therefore, becomes important.

Most children in China, Japan, and Taiwan are expected at an early age to explore ideographs, as well as syllabic and phonetic systems. Repetition, exploration, use of familiar and meaningful symbols, practice, and encouragement are all techniques found in China, Japan, and Taiwan. Teachers and parents guide children into the correct forms and usage, a process which generally takes years.

In conclusion, it is hoped that a view of preschool language interaction in China, Japan, and Taiwan has led the reader to a better understanding of Mandarin,

Japanese, and Fukien and of the expectations held for young children in these three societies. All three complex languages require a lifetime of practice and mastery. Children in China, Japan, and Taiwan are expected to learn more of the spoken vocabulary and less of the written language than one may expect. Japanese view language skills as best taught at home; Chinese emphasize listening and formal speech at school; all three countries require memorization, repetition, and group recitation and ask for less self-expression than Americans.

Through the study of children in preschools, it becomes clear that each effort is well designed to meet the language-learning needs and cultural values of the different countries. Through the study of children in other cultures, one becomes aware of alternatives for learning to read and write.

Different strategies for teaching and differing expectations for children emerge which may motivate us to rethink some of our assumptions about our own preschool language curriculum. The ways children are taught language in preschool are clearly indicative of larger cultural values.

REFERENCES

Anderson-Levitt, Kathryn. Cultural Knowledge for Teaching First Grade: an example from France. To appear in *Toward an Interpretive Ethnography of Education,* G.D. Spindler, ed., LEA, 1987.

Azuma, Hiroshi. "Why Study Child Development in Japan? *In Child Development & Education in Japan,* pp. 1-11.

Bruner, Jerome. "The Language of Education," Reprinted from *Social Research,* Winter 1982, vol. 49, no. 4.

Cooper, Lee. *The Chinese Language for Beginners.* Tokyo, Japan: Chas. E. Tuttle Co., 1984.

Dleland, Craig. Learning to Read: Piagetian Perspectives for Instructions. In *Reading World,* March 1982, pp. 223-224.

Gentry, Joyce. Early Childhood Education in the People's Republic of China. *Childhood Education,* November/December 1981, pp. 92-96.

Kessen, William., ed. *Childhood in China.* New Haven, Conn.: Yale University Press. 1975.

Lewis, Catherine C. Cooperation and Control in Japanese Nursery Schools. In *Comparative Education Review,* February 1984, pp. 69-84.

McElroy, Colleen W. *Speech and Language Development of the Preschool Child,* Charles Thomas, Publisher, Springfield, Ill., 1972.

Rosenbaum, Arthur L. Chinese Education: Reading, Rote and Regimentation? In *47th Yearbook,* Claremont Reading Conference, 1983, pp. 110-117.

Shigaki, Irene S. Childcare Practices in Japan and the United States: how do they reflect cultural values in young children? In *Young Children,* NAEYC, vol. 38, no. 4, May 1983, pp. 13-24.

Shoji, Masako. Early Childhood Education in Japan: Chapter four in *Comparative Early Childhood Education.* Charles C. Thomas, Publisher, Ill., 1983, pp. 48-75.

Stevenson, Harold, Ying Lee and others. Learning to Read Japanese. In *Child Development and Education in Japan,* Stevenson, Azuma, Hakuta, (eds.) N.Y.: W.H. Freeman and Co., 1986, pp. 217-238.

Stevenson, Harold W., J.W. Stigler, Shin-Yin Lee, G.W. Lucker, S. Kitamura, C. Hsee. "Cognitive Performance and Academic Achievement of Japanese, Chinese and American Children in *Child Development,* vol. 56, no. 3, University of Chicago Press, June 1985.

Stewing, John W. *Exploring Language with Children;* Columbus, Ohio: Chas. E. Merrill Publishing Co., 1974.

Tobin J., Davidson, D. and Wu, D. Ratios and Class Size in Japanese Preschools. In *Comparative Education Review,* August 1987.

Zhang, Shuyi. For the Healthy Growth of China's 300 Million Children. In *Beijing Review,* May 31, 1982, pp. 19-25.

Immigrants and Elementary Education in the Boston Public Schools, 1820-1920

Robert L. Osgood

During the nineteenth and early twentieth centuries Boston, Massachusetts experienced a period of dramatic growth. The increase in its population and the consequent expansion of the city's boundaries were fueled largely by a tremendous influx of immigrants, most of whom arrived from Europe in a dispirited and impoverished condition. Their presence demanded that Boston's rapidly expanding public education system adjust to the great variety of languages and cultural backgrounds found within so many of its districts. The city's methods of providing elementary education to its immigrant population were many and varied; an awareness of those methods should prove interesting and instructive to those facing similar challenges in thousands of American public elementary schools today.

Immigration to Boston, while occurring to some extent in every year of the city's history, was characterized by two great waves: the first during the 1840s and 1850s, the second from about 1880 to 1914. The first wave consisted primarily of northern European, particularly Irish, citizens; the second included not only these groups but also large numbers from southern and eastern Europe. Native Bostonians responded to the city's newcomers in various ways, ranging from tacit acceptance to open hostility, depending on the nationality. (1) Even so, Boston's school leadership identified and pursued one essential goal in educating immigrants regardless of their origin: to acculturate, that is to Americanize, them as quickly

and as thoroughly as possible. This purpose was stated
as strongly in the mid-nineteenth century as in 1920;
few ever questioned its propriety. Through education
and acculturation, Boston hoped not only to improve the
quality of life in immigrant neighborhoods but also to
make immigrants think and act like ideal American
citizens, to make them assets rather than burdens to
society:

> [Immigrant children] need special care and
> attention in order that they get right ideas of their
> relation to this country and what the city, state,
> and nation are doing to ameliorate the condition of
> all persons who seek a home on our shores. They
> show a strong desire to learn our language, and
> exhibit an earnest purpose to become thoroughly
> Americanized. The importance of the work to be
> done cannot be overestimated. The life of the
> Republic depends upon the virtue and intelligence
> of the people. (2)

Through the 1800s and early 1900s, Boston's public
schools grew along with the city, frequently
reorganizing curriculum and administration to
accommodate the ever increasing number of native and
foreign-born students. Of great importance to the
system's development were the continuous efforts of
school officials to accomplish the purposes of immigrant
schooling while concurrently responding to the
fundamental daily struggles inherent in teaching a
multicultural student population. Their efforts led to the
incorporation of several educational programs which
reached thousands of first- and second-generation
immigrants: disciplinary schools to "correct" truants
and youthful criminals, kindergartens to benefit
impoverished preschoolers, manual training to hone
motor skills, and industrial education to prepare
students for employment upon leaving school. However,
these programs arose essentially as school responses to
more generalized social concerns — crime, poverty,
urbanization, public health, a rapidly industrializing
economy, educational reform — which were
significantly but by no means exclusively associated
with the phenomenon of immigration. (3) Thus, they

constituted influential but indirect elements in Boston's broad plan to instruct immigrants and their children. To cope directly with the very real problems which a multilingual, multinational student body presented, the Boston public schools established two programs with classroom instruction of non-English-speaking students specifically in mind: the ungraded class and the elementary evening school. In these two settings occurred the city's frontline attempts to transform untrusted immigrants into patriotic Americans.

The origin of the ungraded class can be traced to the 1820s. At that time school regulations restricted enrollment in the newly established primary schools to children seven years old or younger, while the grammar schools required reading and writing ability for admission. As a result, hundreds of Boston's illiterate children were in effect barred from public schooling. School officials, noting that such children generally came from poorer families recently arrived from rural New England or overseas, took action. In 1838, after years of experiment and discussion, the Boston Primary School Board authorized separate " intermediate schools," or "schools for special instruction," in districts where they were deemed necessary, usually in immigrant neighborhoods. Using the prescribed primary school curriculum — reading, writing, spelling, and simple arithmetic taught through memorization and recitation — the intermediate schools increased from four in 1838 to 32 by 1854, at which time over 2,000 students representing just under 10 percent of the total elementary population were enrolled. Over the next 25 years the number of intermediate schools varied, averaging around 20 each year. Eventually coming to believe that intermediate students would benefit from more thorough integration with regular pupils, the Boston School Committee discontinued the schools in 1879, transferring their children into the newly organized classification of the ungraded class within the grammar schools. (4)

The change in name and administrative category did little to alter the character of the schools themselves. Plagued since their inception with ineffective teaching, inefficient classification of students, and a reputation for serving Boston's most difficult and dangerous public school charges, the intermediate schools had come to be known as the "Botany Bays" of the public education system.* School officials continued to associate this term with the ungraded classes. (5)

Over the next four decades the ungraded class remained the fundamental collector for immigrant public school students who for whatever reason were denied participation in the regular day school classes. Not all ungraded class students were immigrant children — the schools banished many native students there because of negligible academic progress, disruptive in-class behavior, truancy, or advanced age — and certainly not all immigrant children were placed in ungraded classes. Nevertheless, most of these classes were located in school districts serving crowded immigrant neighborhoods. Consequently, the programs for and discussions about this category focused on responding to the extreme cultural variety found within. (6)

Such responses proved difficult to implement successfully, as the problems mentioned earlier continued to affect the ungraded classroom. Textbooks and materials were mostly decrepit castoffs suited more for five-year-old native children than for immigrants as old as 17. Teachers were typically inexperienced and/or incompetent despite repeated assertions by school officials that ungraded classes demanded the most skillful, dedicated instructors. (7) Class sizes were huge throughout the system — averaging 56 students near the turn of the century — and though school regulations limited ungraded class size to 35, they were in fact often much larger and typically included a great variety of languages, especially after 1890. Between 1881 and 1900 the ungraded class population increased from 665 to about 2,400, or approximately 6 percent of grammar school students. In several immigrant neighborhoods ungraded class pupils represented the largest single classification in the graded elementary schools. Supervisor Walter S. Parker noted in 1898 that basic English instruction was the most important task

*Botany Bay was a notorious penal colony in southeast Australia.

in ungraded classes, where students from every
European nation could be found. (8)

Teaching methodology depended entirely on the
teacher's preferences and the assorted needs of each
child, or in other words, whatever seemed to work. The
curriculum stayed quite basic, focusing on learning
simple English skills, a little math, and with manual
training exercises being added after 1890. The image of
an inexperienced teacher trying to instruct 40 or more
children of widely divergent ages, nationalities,
abilities, and demeanors with unstandardized, shoddy
equipment is vivid and profound. Remarkably, teachers
and officials alike commented on the positive, energetic,
dedicated attitudes of immigrant children who seemed
to accomplish much regardless of the various obstacles.
(9)

For many years school officials had realized that the
ungraded classes would accomplish little unless their
students were more rationally classified. In 1896 the
first special classes for mentally handicapped children
were established; other classes for children with other
handicaps followed. In 1906 classes designed
specifically for teaching English to newly arrived
immigrant children — the special English classes —
commenced, with 32 in operation by 1917. Each of these
siphoned off considerable numbers of ungraded class
students. After World War 1, ungraded classes became
much less directly concerned with immigrant education
and eventually faded away altogether. (10)

Direct educational adjustment to immigration in
Boston could be seen on a much larger scale in the form
of elementary evening schools. Following the lead of
many other New England cities, Boston opened its first
elementary evening schools in 1868. They were
established for a specific purpose: to offer elementary
instruction to "such persons as have not yet acquired a
competent education, and yet are unable to avail
themselves of the advantages of the day schools." (11)
These included adults, both native and foreign-born,
who had received no formal education, and children
who because of poverty or other circumstance held jobs
during the day. Echoing the mid-century faith in the

ameliorative effects of public schooling, the State
Superintendent of Schools in 1861 proclaimed that the
evening school "cannot fail of doing much to remove
from society that lower stratum, of which ignorance is
the primitive formation, and from which comes much of
the improvidence, unthrift, poverty, and most of the
vices and crimes which we deplore." The Boston School
Committee emphasized that immigration provided the
primary impetus for creating elementary evening
schools. (12)

The elementary evening schools opened their doors
with a great burst of enthusiasm and optimism. The
term ran from early October to early March. Attendance
was voluntary, but students needed to be at least 14
years old unless gainfully employed. The curriculum
corresponded "as nearly as possible with that of the
primary and grammar schools," with special instruction
when needed; the student-teacher ratio was established
at 20-to-one. The number of elementary evening school
students grew from 544 in the first year to several
thousand after 1890, with the number of schools
fluctuating between 12 and 18 between 1870 and 1920.
In the 1880s the schools underwent substantial reform
to address persistent problems of teacher incompetency,
inadequate texts, highly irregular attendance, and
grossly deficient facilities, all of which developed soon
after the schools' inception. These reforms eased but in
no way eliminated such troubles; they continued in
varying degrees throughout the schools' existence,
especially that of irregular attendance. (13)

As of 1890 elementary evening school students
consisted largely of adult immigrants who voluntarily
attended to gain basic knowledge of English. By then
two evening schools were devoted entirely to teaching
English to German immigrants, while teachers were
hired soon after to offer English instruction to Swedes,
Russians, Armenians, and "one or two other languages"
in other schools. School officials strongly encouraged
poorly educated adults and working children to enroll,
as indicated by the use of widespread advertising in
circulars, leaflets, and local foreign-language
periodicals. By 1900 the evening school was a vital
element of the city's attempts to educate its immigrants.
(14)

Between 1900 and 1920 Boston moved to organize more effectively their schools' efforts to provide for the needs of immigrant students. Realizing that in some evening schools 90 to 95 percent of the pupils had no knowledge of English, the School Committee in 1911 restructured the evening school curriculum, dividing it into three core divisions: A, B, and C. Division B included all students whose primary aim was to learn basic English; pupils were placed in classes according to whether they were literate or illiterate in their native language. The method of instruction was based on a carefully sequenced, drill-oriented approach to language learning, that is, constant repetition in phonics, reading, writing, spelling, and conversation. The program also included information on the responsibilities of citizenship, civic ideals, hygiene, home life, naturalization procedures, and voter registration. The main object was to get pupils to *think* in English as well as attain functional literacy. The efficiency and fidelity of implementing this curriculum of course depended on the individual teacher and probably varied considerably. (15)

Until the outbreak of World War 1 in 1914 elementary evening school enrollment stayed high but then showed a steady decline into the 1920s due to the war and the implementation of restrictive national immigration policies. Until the war the schools had maintained their position on the front lines of immigrant education. However, the continued lack of appropriate standardized texts of decent quality and the expressed concern over the number of registered students attending daily — it usually was less than one-third — indicated that the schools still were not all that officials hoped for. Perhaps the biggest concern could be found in the number of immigrants who took advantage of them. The Boston Finance Commission in 1916 reported that only 8,500 immigrants were registered in evening schools out of a total foreign-born population of 240,000. (16) The elementary evening schools continued operation well after 1920, but with the great drop in immigration their focus shifted toward a more generalized adult education program.

The problem of teaching basic skills to a classroom of students who speak a variety of languages tested teachers in Boston a century ago as it tests teachers throughout America today. Large class sizes, instructors who understandably lack functional literacy in their pupils' different languages, and texts which obviously do not satisfy the individual needs of many children inhibit effective learning in the multilingual classroom for everyone regardless of native language. Boston wrestled for decades with these conditions, but despite attempts to alleviate the difficulties the schools' limited resources permitted such attempts to only go so far.

Today, immigrants possess native languages much different than those of Boston's. Nevertheless, immigrant students present noticeably similar challenges to parents, teachers, and administrators who, like their Boston predecessors, are armed with limited resources but still seek to provide the educational quality foreign-born students need and deserve. If there is any initial lesson to be learned from the Boston experience, it is that contemporary educators are not the first to confront the issues attendant to immigrant education. Chronicled in the records of Boston and dozens of other American cities are invaluable descriptions of efforts to reshape public schools in order to accommodate the variety which accompanies any influx of immigration. These descriptions — those of Boston's ungraded classes and elementary evening schools are but two examples — contain a rich store of information about the assumptions, means, and methods employed in the search for efficient immigrant schooling. They also reveal the enormous complexities involved in identifying and reconciling the purposes, resources, and abilities used in the process. To investigate this history is to benefit from the trials of others: to sympathize with their struggles, learn from their mistakes, avoid their pitfalls, and incorporate their accomplishments wherever possible. In the end, the use of history in planning current immigrant education will help us understand the responsibility as well as the opportunity inherent in the collective instruction of learners from widely divergent backgrounds.

NOTES

1 For a discussion of immigration in Boston, see Oscar Handlin, *Boston's Immigrants* (Cambridge, Mass.: Belknap Press, 1959). See also the chapter on immigration in Stephan Thernstrom, *The Other Bostonians: Poverty and Progress in the American Metropolis, 1880-1970* (Cambridge, Mass.: Harvard University Press, 1973).

2 Report of Walter S. Parker, Supervisor in *Annual Report of the Boston School Committee* (hereafter referred to as BSC *Annual Report),* 1898, Appendix p. 133.

3 Excellent discussion of kindergartens, manual training, and industrial education programs in Boston and throughout the region is in Marvin Lazerson, *Origins of the Urban School: Public Education in Massachusetts, 1870-1915* (Cambridge, Mass.: Harvard University Press, 1971), chapters II-VII.

4 Stanley K. Schultz, *The Culture Factory: Boston Public Schools, 1789-1860* (New York: Oxford University Press, 1973), pp. 268-71; BSC *Annual Report,* 1865, 42-43; ibid., 1879, pp. 9-10.

5 Schultz, pp. 269-70; BSC *Annual Report,* 1879, p. 10; ibid., 1887, Appendix p. 151; ibid., 1890, Appendix pp. 143-44.

6 The general information on which this article's description of ungraded classes is based was taken from public school records, especially the BSC *Annual Report,* the *Annual Report of the Superintendent of the Boston Public Schools,* and their appendices, 1870-1920. For this paragraph see BSC *Annual Report,* 1912, pp. 12-13; Walter S. Parker, in ibid., 1895, Appendix p. 166.

7 See, for example, the report of George H. Conley, Supervisor, in BSC *Annual Report,* 1895, Appendix p. 132.

8 Walter S. Parker, in BSC *Annual Report,* 1898, Appendix p. 131. Statistics taken from the BSC *Annual Reports,* 1881-1900.

9 For example, BSC *Annual Report,* 1912, p. 27; Walter S. Parker, in BSC *Annual Report,* 1895, Appendix p. 166.

10 A synopsis of the status of the various programs splintered off from the ungraded classes is found in a report by Maurice P. White, Assistant Superintendent, in an appendix to the Thirty-third *Annual Report of the Superintendent,* School Document #11, 1914, pp. 188-96.

11 John D. Philbrick, in BSC *Annual Report,* 1874, pp. 360-61.

12 Joseph White, in *Report of the Secretary of the Board of Education* (Massachusetts), 1861, cited in the *Sixth Semi-Annual Report of the Superintendent of the Boston Public Schools,* March 1863, in BSC *Annual Report,* 1863, p. 112; BSC *Annual Report,* 1863, pp. 48-49.

13 The BSC *Annual Report* included in almost every year between 1868 and 1920 a section devoted to a review of the city's evening schools, usually in the appendix. It is from these reviews that the information about the schools in this article is taken. Also see Lazerson, op. cit., pp. 204-23, which discusses Massachusetts' evening schools in general.

14 BSC *Annual Report,* 1888, p. 62; Fourteenth *Annual Report of the Board of Supervisors,* 1892, in BSC *Annual Report,* 1892, Appendix p. 502; BSC *Annual Report,* 1899, pp. 24-25.

15 "A Provisional Course of Study for the Evening Elementary Schools," School Document #10, 1911.

16 Survey Committee of the Boston Finance Commission, 1916, in the Thirty-fifth *Annual Report of the Superintendent,* School Document #19, 1916, p. 24.

Presentation of the Recognition of Merit Award to John Reynolds Gardiner

Joan Blumenstein

When the genesis of a story is legend, and thus by definition, from the oral tradition, it takes thoughtful considered writing to transcribe the spirit and essence of such a story to the printed page. To preserve the flavor of the spoken words takes a complex simplicity. That is not a contradiction in terms. *Stone Fox* reads very simply; its storyline is simple and direct; it is an elemental story of youth and shining purpose in conflict with experience and cold cynicism. However, the achieving of that seeming simplicity *is* a complex arduous exercise in writing, re-writing, and re-working of manuscript.

The legend which John Gardiner heard from Bob Hudson in Hudson's Cafe in Idaho Falls in 1974 has become, here, the story of 10-year-old Willy, living with his grandfather on a small potato farm which affords them a bare living. Then comes the day when grandfather gives up, takes to his bed, and refuses to speak. Willy's love and care and the silent concern of the old sled dog Searchlight is acknowledged only by a slight movement of the old man's hand. The farm is to be taken for the non-payment of taxes — $500. Coincidentally, comes the announcement of a national dog-sled race with a purse of $500.

Willy enters it, for he is sure (with the faith of youth) that he and Searchlight can win, for do not they know the course better than any? When they win, Grandfather will be better again and the farm will be safe. But there also enters the race Stone Fox, a giant

Indian with a team of beautiful Samoyeds. He is a cold, silent, isolated man with a set purpose and no shred of feeling or concern for anything but winning. The race is run, and the ending of that race is the true legend.

Does not every true story of human endeavor have its element of tragedy to point up its pinnacle of joy? Real life is always bittersweet, and our legends and folk literature have never flinched from showing us that the life they mirror is real, both happy and tragic. Very truly has Gardiner caught this elemental concept in his portrayal of Willy: his quest, his antagonist, and the love, loyalty, and sacrifice of the true friend, Searchlight the dog.

Re-reading the early reviews of the book, I found one critic who felt the early stages of the story were slow. I disagree. I think the gradual setting of the stage, the careful building to the climax is well thought out and skillful. It ensures that the cold rush of the wind and the swift passage along the course of the race hits one with immediate adrenalin-driving force.

Children also agree, for this is a story they have taken to themselves. They all feel its touch, for could they not all be Willies? As librarians, we have recommended it with assurance to children and to teachers to read to children. We are confident of its power to please, its ability to heighten the awareness of children and teachers as they share it together in their classrooms.

It is with great pleasure that we honor John Reynolds Gardiner with this Recognition of Merit for his outstanding book *Stone Fox.*

A RECOGNITION OF MERIT

Presented to

John Reynolds Gardiner

honoring

STONE FOX

For its power to please and to heighten the awareness of children and teachers as they have shared the book in their classrooms

Presented by THE GEORGE G. STONE CENTER FOR CHILDREN'S BOOKS

of the CLAREMONT GRADUATE SCHOOL

at the 55th ANNUAL CLAREMONT READING CONFERENCE

1987

Acceptance Statement

John Reynolds Gardiner

To quote Thomas Mann, "I do not believe the author is the best judge of his own work."

Whether this is true or not, we do go through our lives being judged by others.

In grammar school, I was accused of plagiarism."You couldn't have written this." Looking back on it now, my teacher had paid me a compliment.

In high school, I received low marks on my compositions, which were poorly written from a spelling and grammar point of view. I was told,"You will never make it in college English."

They were right. In college, I ended up in dumbbell English, along with the foreign students, who proceeded to get better grades than I did.

With all this "encouragement," I wrote nothing between the ages of 18 and 28. Then my brother dragged me to a television writing course, taught by Wells Root, an instructor who didn't give a hoot about spelling or grammar, and my writing career began.

For the next five years, my stories were rejected by the television producers. Discouraged and about to quit, I wrote this story about a boy and his dog, based on a Rocky Mountain legend. It, too, was rejected, but Martin Tahse, a producer of *After School Specials,* asked if he could pass it along to a publisher he knew in New York. I almost said no.

Luckily for me, publishers have two editors — a story editor (who is interested in the story only) and a copy editor (who is interested in grammar and spelling).

After I had worked with the story editor for a year, my manuscript was sent to the copy editor, who informed me that I had misspelled the word *gotten* like *cotton*. Sure I could have said it was a typo, but it occurred eight times in the manuscript.

Since STONE FOX was published seven years ago, I have received numerous — what I call — satisfaction royalties, which include: teaching a writing class back east at Harvard; being on location during the filming of the STONE FOX movie; and, most recently, receiving a phone call informing me of today's award.

I thank the individuals on the committee for judging STONE FOX deserving of the George G. Stone Recognition of Merit award.

And I thank all of you who have ever given a writer encouragement.

Literature and Literacy

Charlotte S. Huck

One of my colleagues at the university is a comparatively new grandfather. Every time I see him he regales me with stories about Lindsey's "reading." Lindsey is only three years old, but her grandfather is determined that she will learn to read as naturally as she is learning to talk. In order to bring this about he has:

- Put some of her books in every room of the house.
- Mixes her books in with her blocks so she will think of them as toys.
- Built her a sturdy bookcase for her own books.
- Made her a little cart like a supermarket cart so she can wheel her favorite books wherever she goes.

Whenever he comes to visit, Lindsey greets him at the door with "Paw Paw read!"

Lindsey is learning to read naturally with real books which delight her. Her home is flooded with books, she sees her mother reading, her father reading, and her grandfather appears to be some kind of nut about books. There is no doubt in my mind that Lindsey will read long before she goes to school.

Lindsey's environment is similar to the rich literacy environments of the mainstream group reported by Shirley Brice Heath in her *Ways With Words*. (1) In this study Heath details three literacy environments found in the Piedmont Carolinas.

1. The first was the townspeople or mainstream group, both black and white, who created rich literacy environments in which books were a natural part of the families' experiences.
2. The second group she called Roadville, a white working class group who emphasized the skills of

reading such as teaching their children the
alphabet and phonic sounds. They bought coloring
books and workbooks for their children rather than
real books. Reading aloud was limited.

3. The third group was known as Tracton and
consisted of the black working class community.
These children heard much oral language but were
not exposed to reading or writing in their homes.

Despite attendance at the same schools, only the
mainstream children who came from the rich literacy
environments achieved what we would call real literacy.
The Roadville children who had been drilled on skills
tended to do well in reading for their first two years,
then their reading scores went down. The Tracton
children were at the bottom of the class and stayed
there throughout school.

Gordon Wells' longitudinal study of the development
of literacy of children in Bath, England, is reported in
his book *The Meaning Makers.* (2) He too talks about
the importance of the literacy environment of the home.
He describes Rosie, the child who had the lowest scores
on all the tests they administered, and Jonathan who
had the highest scores. Wells attributed the difference
between these children largely to the fact that Rosie had
never heard a story read aloud until she came to school,
while Jonathan, he estimated, had heard over 6000
stories before starting school. Jonathan learned to read
easily and naturally while Rosie encountered real
reading difficulties.

What would we have to do differently if we wanted
our schools to provide the same kind of literacy
environments that supported Lindsey, Jonathan, and
the rest of the mainstream children in the Heath study?

Creating rich literacy environments

First of all, we would want to create rich literacy
environments within each classroom. We want to flood
our schools and classrooms with real books, different
kinds of books, picture books, poetry, information books.
I'm convinced that only real books, in contrast to basal
textbooks, make real readers. We want to create

learning environments in our kindergartens and primary grades which would be similar to that which Lindsey's grandfather created for her. We would want to display books at children's eye level; provide a cozy reading corner that would invite children to read.

There is an old Chinese saying that "what is honored in a country will be taught there." I can walk into any classroom and tell you if books are honored there. Two years ago I visited over 20 first-grade classrooms in which I systematically counted the number of books in the reading centers, described the center, looked for evidence of children's art and writing on display, and marked down the number of literacy events going on. It was a discouraging dreary experience for me.

- Each classroom had about 100 old dirty books thrown on the shelves.
- One teacher had placed them on the fourth shelf of a bookcase which made them impossible for any six-year-old to reach.
- Very little children's work was displayed — no pictures with captions, for example.
- I did see quantities of commercial "teacher store" material including alphabet cards, phonic sounds, holiday decorations.
- In all those visits, I saw one child reading from a trade book.
- Each school had a library and librarian aide. Yet I seldom saw children in the library. Upon questioning, I was told classes went once a week in the afternoons to check out one book.

Most primary teachers spend over one half of the day teaching reading — the skills of reading, not the love of reading. Certainly children in these classrooms had no reason to love reading or to learn to read.

In fact, I think more of our schools fit Heath's (3) description of the Roadville families than the mainstream families. We teach reading, the skills of reading; we drill children on workbook exercises, so they can pass their reading tests. Then we wonder why our children are not readers in third, fourth, and fifth grades, why their test scores go down.

Reading aloud

Besides creating rich literacy environments, what else would we do if we wanted children to learn to read naturally? Certainly we would read aloud to children everyday, several times a day, as often as Jonathan and Lindsey heard stories. Reading aloud is one of the most researched and proven practices in developing literacy.

- Robert Thorndike's (4) study of reading in 15 countries showed that children who came from homes that respected reading and had been read aloud to from an early age were the best readers.
- Margaret Clark's (5) study of *Young Fluent Readers* in Scotland showed that children who read before they came to school came from homes that valued reading. All had been read aloud to by their parents or siblings. One father had *told* wonderful fairy tales every night.
- In our country Dolores Durkin's (6) studies of children who learned to read before they came to school in both New York and California showed the same two factors operating.
- Finally, as we have seen, Gordon Wells (7) attributes much significance to the power of young children's hearing stories read aloud. For in his study, *only* listening to stories at an early age was significantly related to the acquisition of literacy and later reading comprehension at age seven.

What is so powerful about this experience which seems to be true for children throughout the world? First reading aloud provides a time for a child to receive a parent's undivided attention. As he or she snuggles up close to a parent, they are learning to associate reading with love and pleasure.

Second, hearing book language in the context of a story helps a child increase his or her vocabulary. Book language is not the same as every-day conversation. In addition, shared reading between a parent and a child always involves conversation and participation. Ninio and Bruner (8) found one of the first language frames to be the consistent way a mother supports her young child in reading a book aloud. Identifying the picture, labeling, and extending understanding of the concept, the mother and child will talk their way through the making meaning of the text.

Besides developing a rich vocabulary by hearing stories read aloud, the child begins to develop a sense of story. He understands beginnings and endings, the use of past tense, how particular characters might behave. What, for example, to expect from a wolf, a fox, a witch, a princess, a grandmother. Knowing the traditional way these characters behave will help the child predict the action of the story. The child may also be abstracting rules about the structure of a story, learning, for example, that if the first Billy Goat goes tripping over the bridge, so will the second and the third.

Finally, in the process of hearing stories, the child gains much information about book handling and concepts of print. She learns where to begin reading, the directionality of print, what constitutes a word, what Don Holdaway (9) refers to as a literacy set for learning to read. Something Lindsey has at three; something Rosie never had a chance to develop.

Some of you are going to say if all this happens before school, what hope is there after a child has entered school? This is one of the reasons I so like an older study done by Dorothy Cohen (10) but later replicated with the same results by Bernice Cullinan, Angela Jaggar, and Dorothy Strickland. (11) Cohen's study was done in New York City with 20 classes of second graders, 10 were experimental and 10 control. She simply sent a list of books to each of the experimental classes and asked the teachers to read aloud from them everyday. The experimental groups also agreed to do something with those books to make them memorable. They could dramatize the story, retell it, create pictures of their favorite characters, something to cause the children to revisit it. At the end of the year the experimental group was significantly ahead of the control group in reading vocabulary and reading comprehension. Evidently reading aloud to children had helped children learn to read.

One of the best kindergarten/first grade teachers I know had this to say about reading aloud:

I read aloud to my children a lot, a whole lot. I'll
read anywhere from one to three stories at a time.
Sometimes I'll reread a favorite story twice, and I
read four to five times a day. I read to the whole
group and to small groups of four or five children,
and to individual children. While I'm reading to the
group I'll encourage them to join in on the refrains.
With individuals, I may point to the words, talk
about what a word is. Sometimes I'll frame a word
with my hand and put it on the board. I put songs,
poems, and refrains on chart paper, so that
children will try to read them by themselves. And
I'll read stories over and over again, just the way
children hear bedtime stories. It's not unusual for
me to read a book twenty times in one month.(12)

Much of what this teacher does is what Don
Holdaway (13) refers to as "Shared Reading" in which
the teacher uses big books to share a book with a large
group in the same way a parent reads a book to their
child. All the children can see the text; they can chat
about both the story and the print much as parents
would do. As the teacher points to the words, they learn
where to begin on a page and directionality of print.
They may predict the action of the story, join in on the
refrains. When I visited primary schools in New
Zealand, each classroom had many big books of nursery
rhymes, songs, and stories. Pairs of children played at
reading the familiar texts together, acting like readers
until they became readers. In fact, one five-year-old boy
said with a certain amount of awe, "See all those words?
Well, I know what they mean!"

It is equally important to read aloud to older students,
too. This is the period when children go on reading jags,
reading all of Judy Blume's books or those of Lois
Lowery or Betsy Byars or all of a choose-your-own
ending series. I wouldn't want to discourage this kind of
reading; in fact, I would encourage it for wide reading
develops fluency. But I would read aloud to the class
books which they will enjoy but might miss in their own
reading. I'd read fantasy to stretch their imaginations,
books such as LeGuin's "Wizard of Earthsea Trilogy,"
Lloyd Alexander's "Prydain Chronicles," Susan
Cooper's "The Dark Is Rising Series." I'd read historical

fiction and biography to give them a sense of their roots. During this period of celebrating the bicentennial of the Constitution and the 100th anniversary of the building of the Statue of Liberty, I might read one of the many immigrant stories that tell of the people who make up this country. One that I read last summer and thoroughly enjoyed is titled *One-Way to Ansonia* by Judie Angell. Much of it reminds me of *Fiddler on the Roof* if the family in that play had emigrated to New York and their story were continued here. Rose Olshansky, age 10, arrives with her four brothers and sisters. Their father, Moshe, had come earlier to make a place for himself. On the night of their arrival he parcels them out to four families, taking only the youngest to live with him and his new wife. Rose goes to work in a sweatshop making caps. But it was here that she heard about night school and the new union movement. Married at 14, Rose decides to better her life and her child's. Promising to send for her husband later, she gives the conductor the small amount of money she has saved and asks him to buy her a ticket to someplace where there are trees and space. He gives her a one-way ticket to Ansonia, Connecticut. Knowing her courage and perseverance, the reader can't help but feel that this will be the way out of the ghetto for all her family. It would make a superb read-aloud book for fifth or sixth graders.

Time for children to read

If we want children to become fluent readers we must give them time to read, time to practice reading books they select and enjoy. Today children spend pitifully little time reading at home. Anderson and his colleagues writing in *Becoming a Nation of Readers* (14) found the average amount of time fifth graders read outside of school was four minutes per day. What if an Olympic swimmer trained only four minutes a day? I suppose that when I was growing up I read two to three hours a day when I was in fifth grade. I read in the car, at night before I went to bed (and after I went to bed with a flashlight under the covers). I read down on the pier of our cabin, out on the raft. Today children watch television some seven hours and ten minutes a day; they

haven't any time for reading at home. They have to
have time to read in school if they are to become
readers. We shall have to reorder our priorities at school
and provide one half hour to 45 minutes each day for
children to enjoy reading. No longer can we afford to
say, "You may read a book when all your other work is
finished," or some children will never have an
opportunity to read.

This is also the time when children should have a
chance to reread books. One first-grade teacher told me
that she used to be concerned when she saw a child
select the same book and read it over and over again
until she realized that these were the very children who
had begun to read. They had found "their book" which
they felt confident in reading. I don't know about you,
but I know I must have read *The Secret Garden* and
Little Women at least 20 times. I'm convinced that when
children start rereading books, they are well on their
way towards becoming real readers.

In-depth reading

Side by side with wide reading should go in-depth
reading. Literature can develop critical appreciative
readers. One group of ten-year-olds read Elizabeth
Speare's *Sign of the Beaver,* the story of one boy's
survival in the Maine woods in 1768. It is also the story
of the gradual coming together of two cultures, the
white man's and the Indians'. Two Indians nurse and
care for Matt while he recovers from the stings he
received as he attempted to obtain honey from a bee
tree. In gratitude he gives the Old Indian one of two
books his family owns, *Robinson Crusoe,* only to realize
too late that the man cannot read. But the old man
makes him promise to teach his grandson. And so a
proud, arrogant Indian boy comes each day for his
reading lesson while he teaches Matt much more in
return —how to survive in the wilderness. The 10-year-
olds loved the story. They created a model of the Indian
village and the log cabin where Matt lived. They made a
chart listing all the gifts that were exchanged in the
story, both tangible and intangible. And one boy wrote
a moving story of how Matt must have felt when the
Indians moved away and left him all alone. These

children lived through Matt's survival through their discussions and interpretations of this well-written, exciting story.

While this group chose to study one book in depth, they might have divided in small groups and had each group read a survival story such as Jean George's new book, *Water Sky*, or *Julie of the Wolves*, Taylor's *Roll of Thunder, Hear My Cry*, or Voigt's *Homecoming*. Such groups would then have something to share with each other as they all explored survival of various kinds.

Literature across the curriculum

Besides being exposed to quality writing in their study of *Sign of the Beaver*, this book provides much which is historically accurate and enriches the social studies. Literature can enrich every subject taught in the curriculum. I can't imagine studying the Middle Ages without using David MacCauley's superb books which detail the building of a *Castle* and *Cathedral*, or Joe Lasker's beautifully illustrated description of two weddings, one a peasant's son, the other a nobleman's daughter in his book *Merry Ever After*. His new book *Tournament of Knights* captures the pageantry and peril of a boy about to fight in his first tournament. Aliki's *Medieval Feast* describes how you prepared for a king's visit and his party of over 100 guests! History books never provide the details, the feelings of the people the way these do. Certainly, this year's Newbery Award winner, *The Whipping Boy*, would add humor to the study of the Middle Ages. Sid Fleischman based his tale upon one historical fact: young princes did have orphans which were used for the sole purpose of serving as stand-ins for the prince's punishment. Such a tale makes history very lively indeed.

Literature and writing

We are just beginning to appreciate the impact literature can make on the quality of children's writing. One first-grade teacher was disturbed by the banality of her children's dictated stories. She began a unit on folktales with them in which she read the many fairy tales which they had missed including *Cinderella, The*

Sleeping Beauty, and Hodges' book, *Saint George and the Dragon,* with its award winning illustrations by Trina Schart Hyman. Combining their favorite storybook character "Spot" (from Eric Hill's *Where's Spot?)* with all kinds of elements from folktales, the children created their own story titled *Spot the King.* Spot was eaten by a dragon, but he used his magic to get out of the dragon's stomach. Kissed by his queen, he was restored to life. Their story not only contained many elements of fairy tales but the language reflected the hyperbole of folktales. Spot was the "kindest king," married to the "beautifuliest queen." There was no question that hearing many folktales had enriched their language and story-telling capacities.

One sixth-grade teacher regularly selects a poem to go with the book she is reading aloud. It was not unusual, then, for one of her students to *write* a poem when the teacher finished reading aloud Katherine Paterson's well-loved story *Bridge to Terabithia.* You recall this is the story of an unusual friendship between Jess, a local boy from a large family, and Leslie, the highly imaginative daughter of two writers. Isolated in the country, the two find their own special island in the midst of a stream. It is Leslie who suggests they name it "Terabithia" after C.S. Lewis' Narnia stories.

The children had to swing on old rope to get across the stream. One day after a severe rainstorm, Leslie goes there alone. The frayed rope gives way and she is drowned. Let me share with you Cheri's poem which she wrote the night after her teacher finished the story in class.

As the stubborn stream
   swirls and pulls out a song
The hillside stands in the cold dark sky.
Over the hillside stands
   a lovely palace.
Before
   it shook with joy,
But now
   its queen is dead.
So the sour sweet wind
Blows the tassels of the weak rope

And the tree mourns
   scolding the rope, saying
Couldn't you have held out a little longer.

Cheri Taylor (15)

Can literature impact on children's reading and writing? I believe it is as closely intertwined as a well-woven rope. Only when we separate the strands and try to teach the skills of reading or writing in isolation without the support of literature do we fail.

Readers, the Lindseys, the Jonathans of Wells' study, are not born, they are made.

- They are made by parents who love books and read aloud to their children.

- They are made by teachers and librarians who are avid, enthusiastic readers themselves who share books with children and provide time for children to read and respond to books.

- They are made by teachers who encourage children to read and write their own stories, poems, and books rather than fill in blanks in workbooks.

When each classroom becomes a community of readers, then we shall truly become a nation of readers.

REFERENCES

1 Heath, Shirley Brice, *Ways With Words.* Cambridge University Press, 1983.

2 Wells, Gordon, *The Meaning Makers: Children Learning Language and Using Language to Learn.* Heinemann Educational Books, 1986.

3 Heath, op. cit.

4 Thorndike, Robert L., *Reading Comprehension: Education in 15 Countries: An Empirical Study,* Vol. 3, International Studies in Education. Holstead Wiley, 1973.

5 Clark, Margaret, *Young Fluent Readers.* Heinemann Educational Books, 1976.

6 Durkin, Dolores, *Children Who Read Early.* Columbia Teachers College Press, 1966.

7 Wells, op. cit.

8 Ninio, A. and J. Bruner, "The Achievement and Antecedents of Labelling." *Journal of Child Language.* Vol. 5, 1973.

9 Holdaway, Don, *The Foundations of Literacy.* Ashton Scholastic, 1979.

10 Cohen, Dorothy, "The Effect of Literature on Vocabulary and Reading Achievement." *Elementary English 45* (February 1968), 209-13, 217.

11 Cullinan, Bernice E., Angela Jaggar, and Dorothy Strickland. "Language Expansion for Black Children in the Primary Grades: Research Report." *Young Children 29* (January 1974), 98-112.

12 Hepler, Susan (Ed.), *The Best of The WEB.* Center for Reading, Language Arts and Children's Literature, College of Education, Ohio State University, 1982.

13 Holdaway, op. cit.

14 Anderson, Richard C., *et al., Becoming a Nation of Readers* (Washington: National Institute of Education), 1984.

15 Huck, Charlotte, Susan Helper, and Janet Hickman, *Children's Literature in the Elementary School,* 4th edition, Holt, Rinehart and Winston, 1987, p. 393.

BIBLIOGRAPHY — CHILDREN'S BOOKS

Alcott, Louisa M. *Little Women,* illustrated by Barbara Cooney, Crowell, 1955 (1868).

Alexander, Lloyd. "The Prydain Chronicles"
    The Book of Three, Holt, 1964.
    The Black Cauldron, Holt, 1965.
    The Castle of Llyr, Holt, 1966.
    Taran Wanderer, Holt, 1967.
    The High King, Holt, 1968.

Aliki (Brandenberg). *A Medieval Feast.* Crowell, 1983.

Angell, Judie. *One-Way to Ansonia.* Bradbury Press, 1985.

Brown, Marcia. *The Three Billy Goats Gruff.* Harcourt, 1972.

Burnett, Frances Hodgson. *The Secret Garden,* illustrated by Tasha Tudor. Lippincott, 1962 (1911).

Cooper, Susan. "The Dark Is Rising" Series. Atheneum.
    Over Sea, Under Stone, 1966.
    The Dark Is Rising, 1973.
    Greenwitch, 1974.
    The Grey King, 1975.
    Silver on the Tree, 1977.

Fleischman, Sid. *The Whipping Boy,* illustrated by Peter Sis. Greenwillow, 1986.

George, Jean Craighead. *Julie of the Wolves,* illustrated by John Schoenherr. Harper, 1972.

_____ *Water Sky.* Harper, 1987.

Hill, Eric. *Where's Spot?* Putnam, 1980.

Hodges, Margaret, *Saint George and The Dragon,* illustrated by Trina Schart Hyman. Little, Brown, 1984.

Hutton, Warwick. *The Sleeping Beauty.* Atheneum, 1979.

Lasker, Joe. *Merry Ever After: The Story of Two Medieval Weddings.* Viking, 1976.

LeGuin, Ursula K. "Earthsea Trilogy." Atheneum.
    A Wizard of Earthsea, 1968.
    The Tombs of Atuan, 1971.
    The Farthest Shore, 1972.

Lewis, C.S. "The Narnia Series," Macmillan.
    The Lion, The Witch, The Wardrobe, 1961.
    The Horse and His Boy, 1962.
    The Silver Chair, 1962.
    The Voyage of the "Dawn Treader," 1962.
    The Magician's Nephew, 1964.
    Prince Caspian, The Return to Narnia, 1964.
    The Last Battle, 1964.

MacCaulay, David. *Castle.* Houghton Mifflin, 1977.

    —————— *Cathedral.* Houghton Mifflin, 1973.

Paterson, Katherine. *Bridge to Terabithia,* illustrated by Donna Diamond. Crowell, 1977.

Perrault, Charles. *Cinderella,* illustrated by Marcia Brown. Scribner, 1954.

Speare, Elizabeth George. *The Sign of the Beaver.* Houghton Mifflin, 1983.

Taylor, Mildred. *Roll of Thunder, Hear My Cry.* Dial, 1976.

Voigt, Cynthia. *Homecoming.* Atheneum, 1981.

"One of Us, One of Us, We Will Make You One of Us"

Abbie Shuford Prentice

Children read pictures. Children read pictures before they read print. They read gestures and facial expressions and body language — all before they read printed words. Reading images, then, is a way of knowing. "This point of view regards reading as the process of creating meaning for a variety of sensed stimuli, of which the act of reading print is an integral part." (1)

Children read pictures as "primary reading." (2) Peter L. Spencer has stated that reading behavior is divided into two major parts: primary and secondary reading. Primary reading is the direct experiencing of contact with one's environment. "It then refers to reading-behavior which is *basic* or *fundamental* to the advancement of effective adaptive responding." (3) *"Secondary reading* is characterized by indirect or vicarious experiencing by means of symbols. It is so named because it depends upon, or is secondary to, the primary reading of things." (4)

It can then be hypothesized that when children "read" pictures in a picture storybook, a response will follow. MacCann and Richard believe this response can be remarkable and they state: "As part of the young child's environment, picture books can have a profound effect upon his whole pattern of development." (5)

To evaluate all of what children perceive when they read a picture book would be an impossible task. Children have neither the experience nor the vocabulary to interpret and completely describe all their responses to such stimuli. However, children do form attitudes and opinions while quite young. They demonstrate racial prejudices and sex-role bias before they are secondary readers of print and before they have the semantic knowledge of the words or the articulation skills to verbalize them.

The study described here examined the stimuli presented to children in picture books. It asked the question: "What do children read in picture books?"

Subjects

The Caldecott Medal Award books, from 1938 through 1983, comprise the subjects of this study. Arbuthnot, et al., (6) have described Caldecott Medal books as the very best picture storybooks for children from two to seven years old. Irene Smith has stated that Caldecott Medal books set standards rather than cater to them; therefore, excellence in content and design can be fairly placed in their direct line of influence. (7)

Data gathering procedures

Nine Content Analysis Forms were designed to record the existence of selected behaviors, attitudes, and environmental surroundings presented in text and illustrations in the Caldecott books. They sought to identify, tabulate, and analyze information about the following: Behaviors of Children, Behaviors of Parents, Home Environment, Male Sex-role Behaviors,* Story Endings, Portrayal of Black Characters, African Characters, Hispanic, and Asian Characters.

To determine the relative circulation statistics of the Caldecott Award books, a count was made in each of the regional libraries and 20 percent of the branch libraries of the Los Angeles County Library system. Care was taken to choose branch libraries which would give a sampling of the readership population with regard to socio-economic level of the neighborhood, ethnic population, geographic location, and size of the library. When all circulation data had been collected, the books

---

*Only male sex-role behaviors were investigated. Female sex-roles were investigated in a dissertation by Patricia Roberts.

were placed in rank order ranging from the most to the least widely circulated in each library, in each region, in the entire sample.

Findings

Behaviors of Children. Of all the 46 Caldecott books subjected to analysis, in only two were children rude to adults while only two children were naughty. Lazy Mary, in *The Rooster Crows,* told her mother she would not get out of bed. Mary was not punished or repentant.

Max, in *Where the Wild Things Are,* was both rude and naughty. He told his mother he would eat her up and made mischief of one kind and another. He was sent to bed without eating anything, but upon arrival in his room he proceeded to make the trip to the land of the wild things. He did not go to bed, and when he tired of the wild things and was hungry, he came back home to find "his supper waiting for him and it was still hot." Naughty Max, not punished, not repentant.

The Bad Kangaroo, in *Fables,* put thumbtacks on the teacher's chair, threw spitballs across the classroom, set off firecrackers in the lavatory, and spread glue on the doorknobs. When the principal went to visit Mr. and Mrs. Kangaroo, he found the parents also enjoyed doing the same things at home. Since the parents did not think their child was naughty, he was not punished.

Mei Li ran off to the Fair when she knew girls were not supposed to go. When she was brought home by her uncle, she was greeted warmly by her mother. The fact that she had broken a rule was never mentioned by her mother, and Mei Li was not punished.

Behaviors of Parents. Three parents were rude to children. Max's mother, in *Where the Wild Things Are,* called him a WILD THING. Cinderella's stepmother gave her the vilest household tasks. The mother of the Fool of the World called him "Stupid fellow," and when he told her he was going to leave home to seek his fortune, she "put in the bag some crusts of black bread and a flask of water," not the soft white rolls, several kinds of cooked meats, and bottles of corn brandy which she gave to her other two sons when they left home. It should also be mentioned that Cinderella's stepmother was the only parent who was rude to her spouse.

In none of the Caldecott books did a parent refuse the help of a child, and only two parents expressly disliked the actions of a child. Max's mother sent him to his room, and Sam's father, in *Sam, Bangs & Moonshine,* scolded her for making up stories. Two children were verbally and/or physically abused by their parents: The Fool and Cinderella. The Fool seemed not to care and Cinderella forgave everyone.

Home Environment. Twenty books portrayed two parents in a home setting, and while it was implied in some books that the children were living with both parents, in only two was the absence of a parent explained. The mother in *Chanticleer and the Fox* and the father in *Sam, Bangs & Moonshine* were both widowed. In eight books, adults either smoked tobacco or the drinking of alcohol was mentioned. No book had women in curlers and only *They Were Strong and Good* showed men unshaven.

Cinderella was dressed in rags and called "filthy Cinderseat," but the illustrations belie the words for she is clean and well-groomed throughout. Three other books illustrate children in torn clothing: the black children in *The Rooster Crows;* the boy soldier and slaves in *They Were Strong and Good;* and Abe, his sister, and the slaves in *Abraham Lincoln. The Funny Little Woman* stays clean even when she falls down in the mud. There may be a hint of mud on her when she comes out of the hole in the ground, but none on her hands. The brown "mud color" is so subtle that it is difficult to tell if the illustrator is actually depicting mud or an artistic water color wash. All 46 books show neat, well-groomed people.

Male Sex-Role Behaviors. Whenever males and females of the same age group are pictured standing, the males are taller most of the time. Of the 27 books to which this item applied, 23 pictured the male taller. Sixteen books had rich/or powerful males, and 14 books presented the male as the family provider and protector. Males nosed out females as being the oldest or only child in a family by 16 to 13, but in 42 books, males were portrayed as having high self-esteem.

Story Endings. Forty-three of the 46 books had happy endings. *Fables,* a compilation of stories, had at least one story to fit all four categories and was the only book judged as having a sad-ending story.

Portrayal of Black Characters. The Snowy Day is the only Caldecott book in which all the characters are black. In *Abraham Lincoln* the only blacks are slaves, and as characters, less than essential to the plot. Only once do they speak: "Glory, glory hallelujah" as Lincoln walks by. Dick, the slave in *They Were Strong and Good,* has no lines; neither does the minstrel in *Many Moons.* In fact, there is only one small picture of the minstrel.

Ten categories of stereotypical items were found in the five Caldecott books that portray blacks: slaves content with status; pictured with farm, cleaning, or cooking tools, weapons; protecting/serving well-groomed whites, especially children; barefoot, torn clothing; wearing bandana, overalls, apron, or calico; obese women, skinny children; matriarchal family; coal black skin; minstrel; and dialectical speech. The illustrations of blacks was found to be less than flattering in all of the books.

When *The Rooster Crows* was awarded the Caldecott Medal in 1946, the original edition had two pages showing coal black, skinny, barefoot children, one shivering in the snow, the other in front of a shanty, and both speaking black dialect. Public opinion was so aroused that 18 years later a new edition was published completely deleting the black children, leaving an all-white world of children. In an article titled "The All-White World of Children's Books," Nancy Larrick discussed white supremacy in children's literature:

> Why are they always white children? The question came from a five-year-old Negro girl who was looking at a picturebook at the Manhattenville Nursery School in New York. With a child's uncanny wisdom, she singled out one of the most critical issues in American education today: the

almost complete omission of Negroes from books
for children. Integration may be the law of the
land, but most of the books children see are all
white. (8)

Although Larrick was speaking of portrayals of black
and white characters in books, any ethnic minority can
be substituted for the word Negro, and the meaning
would be the same. Picture books are a white world —
few blacks, few Hispanics, few Asians, few native
Americans.

Portrayal of African Characters. Four Caldecott
Award books were set in Africa with black Africans as
the characters. All four books portrayed black Africans
as living in the bush, jungle, forest, or primitive
villages. All African books described the people as
superstitious with no formal education. The characters
lived in huts and lean-to's, wore scant clothing, loin
cloths and sometimes animal skins. Tribal activities
were dancing and story telling. Beads and rings on
ankles adorned the tribal members, and each book
pictures characters carrying spears, shields, or clubs. In
Shadow and *Ashanti to Zulu,* the people are nomads
who hunted and fished for food, cooked and warmed
themselves over campfires, while the women carried
packages on their heads. Nowhere were cities drawn, no
schools, no streets, no houses. Since no one was
formally educated, no professionals were seen, no
doctors, lawyers, teachers, bankers, statesmen. No
artists, carpenters, plumbers, chefs, storekeepers were to
be seen. If readers believe this is Africa, the great city of
Nairobi would be an impossibility.

Portrayal of Hispanic Characters. Two books, *Nine
Days to Christmas* and *Song of the Swallows,* portray
Mexican people. Both books climax with a fiesta where
the children sing and dance. Sex-roles are clearly
defined in *Nine Days to Christmas.* The father goes off
to work in an office and Ceci is left with her mother,
baby brother, and the maid. Women are depicted doing
chores of cleaning, marketing, cooking, emptying the
garbage (which is the big event of the day for the
servant girls who flirt with the garbage collectors), and
nurturing children.

In *Song of the Swallows,* Juan is told the legend of the birds and the missionaries of Capistrano by old Julian. It is the story of Father Junipero Serra and the brothers who founded the mission and taught the poor Indians to make "things they need in their daily life." It causes the reader to wonder how the Indians existed before Catholicism. Nine stereotyping images were illustrated in both books.

Portrayal of Asian Characters. Mei Li is the story of a Chinese girl who runs off to the Fair, something that girls are not supposed to do. She walks behind her older brother and is too frightened to shoot off firecrackers. Fearful of not hitting the good luck bell with her penny, she asks her brother to throw it for her. Uncle Wang talks "of the sights to be seen in the city." Mei Li listens "sadly because... girls always had to stay home... If I always stay home, what can I be good for?" She had watched her mother "baking and frying and chopping," so she probably had some idea of what she was good for. Mei Li's hair is worn in a "candletop." Dressed in the ethnic coat and pants of Chinese peasants, she is superstitious, weak, and subordinate to males.

Another Asian character is drawn in *The Funny Little Woman.* She, too, is portrayed as subordinate to males. Kidnapped by the fanged, male creature called an oni, and taken to a strange house where she is forced to cook for all the onis while held captive, she laughs: "tee-he-he-he-he!" She claims she will have fun for weeks cooking rice dumplings. She does outwit the oni and escapes with a magic rice paddle which is credited for greatly helping to make her the richest woman in all of Japan. But, she leaves behind a memory of a little Japanese woman dressed in a kimono, chopsticks in her hair, bowing to males, doing their bidding, and laughing.

Circulation Data. If recency were a factor of circulation, then the results of the data should show the books published in the seventies and eighties to be the most widely circulated, and books published in the thirties and forties to be the least circulated. However, *The Little House,* 1942, and *Make Way for Ducklings,* 1941, are second and fourth, respectively, while *A Tree*

Is Nice, 1956, and *The Snowy Day,* 1962, are third and fifth in circulation. *Where the Wild Things Are,* 1963, was found to be the most circulated book of all. Therefore, recency does not appear to be a factor.

Two libraries surveyed in the present study were described in the U.S. 1980 Census Table as being in predominately black areas and showed *Where the Wild Things Are* to be the most widely circulated of all the Caldecott books. *The Snowy Day,* fifth in the total sample, was second and third in circulation, respectively, of the two libraries. Neither placed one of the books about black Africans in the top five of their circulation.

The service areas of six of the libraries surveyed were composed of 5-to-15 percent Asian Pacific people. Five of the six showed *Where the Wild Things Are* as first in the individual rank order, and three libraries placed *Mei Li* in the five least circulated books. No library placed *The Funny Little Woman* in the five most circulated books, and two libraries showed this book among the five least circulated.

Seven libraries were located in predominately Hispanic neighborhoods. One library did not own a copy of *Where the Wild Things Are,* but five placed this title in the five most circulated, and one library tallied the book in sixth place. *Song of the Swallows* was among the five least circulated books in five of the seven libraries, and only one library placed *Nine Days to Christmas* in the five most circulated books.

Thus, it appears that neither timeliness in terms of publication date, nor the ethnic composition of a neighborhood, could be considered a factor in circulation. Caldecott books with ethnic characters had no higher circulation in like ethnic neighborhoods than in any other community. *Where the Wild Things Are* cut across all racial differences, socioeconomic levels, and geographic locations. It was consistently the highest in circulation. Also, the five most circulated books from the rank order of the entire sample showed among the top 10 books in each individual library with harmonious regularity.

Summary

In the study reported here, Caldecott Award books show disturbing patterns in their portrayal of children, families, environments, and story endings. Few books have ethnic minorities as characters, and when a black is included in a book, often no lines are ascribed to that character. Parents and children do not quarrel with each other, and rarely do they disagree or do children disobey. Only Max, *Where the Wild Things Are*, raised his voice to his mother.

No family was homeless. Families were depicted in a happy light, with strong secure bonds. Some children had important responsibilities, but for the most part, childhood was a carefree, happy time with fun things to do. No child disliked his parents, and the classic sibling rivalry was nonexistent. Children stayed clean even when playing in the dirt; in fact, 100 percent of the Caldecott books show neat, well-groomed people. Children swing in trees, jump off rocks, run and play, with never a skinned knee or a tangle in their hair.

The word, divorce, was not mentioned in any of the 46 books, and death, a reality we all face, was not addressed. Except for the four naughty children mentioned earlier, Caldecott children are good. They are also nice, sweet, kind, forgiving, generous, sympathetic, happy, considerate, and helpful. They bring gifts to their parents (*The Girl Who Loved Wild Horses*); they thank God for their parents (*Prayer for a Child*); they respect their grandparents (*The Egg Tree*) and kindly adults (*Song of the Swallows*); they have parties and fiestas (*May I Bring a Friend, Nine Days to Christmas, Song of the Swallows*). They enjoy picnics (*A Tree Is Nice*) and spend their summers at their other home on the island where they swim, sail, and play until it is time to go back to school (*Time of Wonder*).

Children have responded by showing a clear preference for Max, the naughty boy who is yelled at by his mother, replies in kind, and in the end, forgiven by a mother "who loved him best of all." Perhaps Max appeals to children because he says things that all children say, or wish they could say and get away with it. Or maybe, the imagination of children is captured by the wild things that are tamed by Max. Perhaps the developmental factors and characteristics of children's thinking which were present in his story have made the difference in circulation.

What do children read in picture books? If they read Caldecott books, they see a perfect world with perfect, white children. In the land of Caldecott, no child is deaf or hard of hearing. No one wears eyeglasses. No parent knew the heartbreak of having a child with a birth defect, and no child knew the pain of growing up "different." What, then, is the meaning children create for these sensed stimuli?

Without regard for recency of publication or ethnic composition of the characters, children checked out *Where the Wild Things Are* twice as many times as even the next four books in the study, and they returned it to the libraries less times than any other book. There appeared to be some reluctance to relinquish the book, and the hero was a naughty boy.

In the film, *Invasion of the Body Snatchers,* the aliens descended upon Earth with the purpose of changing every human into like clones. As they carry out their assignments, they chant: "One of us, one of us, we will make you one of us." It has been said Caldecott Award books set standards rather than cater to them, but is there a "set Caldecott child?" Is there a connecting, subliminal thread of a message stitching the books together as a body of work — a message to children: "Be good, be clean, be perfect, be one of us?"

Children are not born with attitudes toward races, sex-role opinions, and positions on family relationships; these fall into the category of learned behaviors. David Gast concurs:

> Social scientists...generally agree that there are
> no inherent cultural predispositions of traits among
> people of different races or geographical areas, but
> that man is a product of his cultural environment.
> The shaping of this product begins at birth.
> Children literally "learn what they live." (9)

Picture books pack a powerful punch. It is also possible,
to paraphase Gast, that children "learn what they
read."

REFERENCES

1 Malcolm P. Douglass, (1972). "Introduction to the Yearbook," *36th
   Yearbook of the Claremont Reading Conference*. Claremont,
   Calif.: The Claremont Graduate School, p. 2.

2 Peter L. Spencer, (1970). *Reading Reading,* Alpha Iota Chapter. Pi
   Lambda Theta: Claremont, Calif., p. 75.

3 *Ibid.,* p. 66.

4 *Ibid.,* p. 83.

5 Donnarae MacCann and Olga Richard, (1973). *The Child's First
   Books — A Critical Study of Pictures and Texts*. New York: The H.
   W. Wilson Company.

6 May Hill Arbuthnot, Dorothy M. Broederric, Shelton L. Root, Jr.,
   Mark Taylor and Evelyn L. Wenzel, (1981). *The Arbuthnot
   Anthology of Children's Literature,* Third Edition. Glenview,
   Illinois: Scott, Roresman and Company, p. 1079.

7 Irene Smith, (1957). *A History of the Newbery and Caldecott
   Medals*. New York: The Viking Press, p. 104.

8 Nancy Larrick, "The All-White World of Children's Books." *the
   Saturday Review,* 48:63, September 11, 1965, p. 63.

9 David Gast, "Minority Americans in Children's Literature."
   Elementary English, January 1967, p. 12.

When I was little I used to play a lot. . .*

Gretchen H. Reynolds

Introduction

When teachers were asked to brainstorm why they value play, the list included the following reasons. In play, children. . .

think creatively,

practice critical thinking,

use problem solving skills,

teach themselves,

are independent,

have power,

have control over the environment,

are cooperative,

don't need rewards or punishments,

have fun,

and are totally involved.

Discussions on play have a magnetic attraction for teachers. Teachers in the primary grades want their classrooms to be playful places and are frustrated by the discrepancy between what they would like and what they know the reality to be. Good teachers are careful observers of children. By watching children, they know that the involvement and spontaneity which they see in children, at free time or recess, are often lacking during much of the academic portion of the school day.

There is mounting pressure on the schools to improve academic conditions. Contemporary pedagogical theory

---

* — Piaget (1932, p. 24).

reflects this concern by asking teachers to spend more time teaching skills through direct instruction and practice. Teachers in first and second grades, and kindergarten and preschool as well, are feeling the impact of this pressure. Many primary classrooms have no time for play unless it can be rationalized as reinforcing skills, and then usually it takes the form of computer programs and flashcard competition. Kindergartners in some schools must pass qualifying tests to enroll in first grade. There are preschool programs based on the deficit model of instruction. Developmental tests are administered to children to find out what is wrong or lacking. Attempts are made to fix the problem by teaching children what they do not know.

These kinds of practices are glaringly inappropriate for very young children. Currently in the United States there is a move to provide universal preschool education for four-year-olds. Where there is little debate that public preschool would be socially advantageous for a number of reasons, the dilemma is what constitutes appropriate programming (Zimilies, 1986). A fear is that traditional teaching methods will be increasingly emphasized in preschool education: "What are the gains and losses for a child exposed to a prescribed set of skills and facts that it is obligatory to learn? What does it mean to the young child to fail to live up to expectations, to be asked and be unable to perform certain tasks or learn certain concepts? What are the enduring consequences of having to adapt to an environment that may be perceived as unfriendly and/or to experience early failure?" (Zimilies, 1986, p.191).

The emphasis on high academic standards does not mean that traditional teaching methods are suitable for all ages of children. Nor does it guarantee that children will know more if we start instructing them sooner.

In this article I will argue for the reverse trend: time for play needs to be incorporated into each school day at the preschool, kindergarten, and primary grade levels. The particular kind of play I will be discussing is sociodramatic play. Symbolic play (sociodramatic play is one form) develops after the child develops the ability to articulate clearly, between the ages of two and four. Between four and seven this kind of play becomes increasingly complex. During the ages of seven to eleven play gradually becomes reality focused (Piaget, 1960).

Sociodramatic play defined

The following is Smilansky's (1968) definition of sociodramatic play:

> In dramatic play the child takes on a role: he pretends to be somebody else. While doing this he draws from his first- or secondhand experience with the other person in different situations. He initiates the person, in action and speech, with the aid of real or imagined objects. The verbalization of the child during play is imitated speech or serves as substitute for objects, action, and situations. The play becomes sociodramatic if the theme is elaborated in cooperation with at least one other roleplayer; then the participants interact with each other both in action and verbally. Some of the verbal interaction is imitation of adult talk, and an integral part of the role playing; some is verbal substitution for objects, actions, and situations, directed to the coplayers, and some of it constitutes discussions necessary to play and sustain the cooperative play (p. 7).

Smilansky's (1968) study was conducted in Jerusalem, Israel, with the children of immigrants from various Middle Eastern and North African countries. These children consistently failed to meet scholastic criteria in first grade, which seemed to establish a pattern of continuing lack of success in later grades. The goal of the work at the H. Szold Institute for Research in Behavioral Sciences was to develop a "... program of intellectual promotion that will facilitate a child's successful participation in the primary grades at school" (p. 2).

Smilansky's notion was that when children play in cognitively advanced ways they are using a similar kind of symbolic thinking that is required in school. Unfortunately Smilansky did not test this hypothesis.

She did attempt to verify that children could learn how to play in cognitively advanced ways. The type of play that was selected to be taught to the children was sociodramatic play, not only because of its complexity, but also because it was considered to be a natural form of play for children.

Smilansky developed six criteria by which to judge the cognitive complexity of sociodramatic play. They are imitative role play, make-believe with objects, make-believe in regard to actions and situations, persistence in the play for more than 10 minutes, the interaction of at least two players, and verbal interaction among the players related to the play episode.

Pellegrini: the relationship between kindergartners' play and achievement in prereading, language, and writing

Pellegrini (1980) studied the relationship between play and kindergartners' achievement on tests for prereading, language, and writing. The children were 65 kindergartners from mixed socioeconomic backgrounds in rural Georgia. They were administered the Metropolitan Reading Test for prereading and language skills and a second test for writing fluency. The children also were observed during free play for five 20-minute periods. Their play was ranked on a continuum (Smilansky, 1968) of four levels reflecting incremental degrees of cognitive complexity. The categories of play, from simplest to most complex, were: functional play, in which the child simply exercises her muscles; constructive play, which is creative activity involving several kinds of actions with the formation of a structure as a goal; dramatic play, which involves symbolic play and language in a common enterprise; and games-with-rules, where play is subordinated to a preconditional set of rules.

Pellegrini found a high significance of correlation and prediction between play and the achievement variables: prereading, language, and writing fluency. Of the four categories of play, in a test of main effects, sociodramatic play showed the highest effect on the variables. There were no instances of games-with-rules, suggesting that these findings were the result of the transference of children's symbolic behavior in play to competency with symbols in reading and writing.

Smilansky's and Pellegrini's studies pose some interesting questions for further research, selected for this article because of the similarities of the hypotheses of each with the concepts in Vygotsky's developmental theory.

Vygotsky's theory of development: the historical-dialectical framework

Vygotsky worked at the Institutes of Psychology and Defectology in Moscow for the 10 years prior to his death in 1934. He was strongly influenced by the political philosophies of Marx and Engels, applying the tenets of dialectical and historical materialism to his psychological theory. His view of development concurs with that of his contemporary, Piaget, that there are patterns and stages of child development. But the Soviet's theory incorporates the broader influence of historical conditions on the growing individual; no two persons' experiences are identical because of the constantly changing nature of historical opportunities.

Engels' dialectic thinking and notions of how man uses labor and tools to transform the external environment are also highly evident in Vygotsky's psychology. He extends Engels' notion of tool use to sign systems: language, writing, and number systems, which are created by societies and internalized by developing members of the culture. The tools and signs of a culture enable individuals not only to affect and change their environments but also to create new conditions for living.

Vygotsky's theory is built on the theme that human behaviors first occur externally, gradually developing to internalized functions. This structure is evident in one concept I will explore in depth shortly: the evolution from somatic motion in toddlers to the use of symbol in middle childhood. Another example of this theme in Vygotsky is his idea that thinking is language which has become internalized. A third concept is the

development of self-regulation: very young children
need the support of adults to keep them in control.
Gradually children acquire the ability to behave
autonomously, with an internalized sense of appropriate
behaviors, both social and moral.

The zone of proximal development. Vygotsky
contends that pedagogy is only effective when it is
appropriately in advance of the child's development;
anything that is beneath her current level of
development, such as a task that is repetitious or
mundane, is of no significance. The task of the educator,
thus, is to create learning experiences which provide
suitable challenges for the child. The most appropriate
match Vygotsky called "the zone of proximal
development." It is the distance between the actual
developmental level as determined by independent
problem solving and the level of potential development
as determined through problem solving under adult
guidance or in collaboration with more capable peers."
(1978, p. 86). Within a zone of proximal development,
appropriate learning experiences evoke the child's
emerging capacities: "what a child can do with
assistance today she will be able to do by herself
tomorrow, a process by which children grow into the
intellectual life of those around them" (pp. 87-88). The
two types of situations for school-age children which
establish the zone of proximal development are:
thoughtful questioning by an adult who guides
children's thinking, and collaboration with more
capable peers.

Vygotsky's recommendations for pedagogy are
supported by interesting research in primary
classrooms in England (Sylva, in Cazden, 1980).
Researchers hoped to clarify characteristics of school
environments which supported children's complex
behaviors. Complex action, or action requiring cognitive
complexity, was coined as "cognitive stretch" (Cazden,
1980, p. 10). Research results indicated that the greatest
cognitive stretch occurred during dialogues between
pairs of children who were engaged in collaborative
problem solving.

The place of play. Vygotsky contends that for preschoolers, play creates the zone of proximal development. Good play stretches children cognitively. The following diagram representing his theory illustrates the path of development in the child from sensorimotor gesture, which is external, through drawing and symbolic play, to the internal processes of symbolic functioning with written sign (Emig, 1983, p. 138).

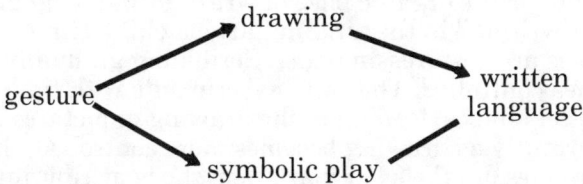

Gesture, requisite for all further development, is any motoric behavior of the very young child; it is analogous to the sensorimotor activity of toddlers who learn through movement and by exploring (Piaget, 1962). Preschool age children develop competency in symbolic functioning through drawing and symbolic play. These are first-order symbols. This age is transitional to symbolic functioning on a more abstract level, or second-order symbolization, when the child creates a symbol to represent a symbol, such as a written word, to designate a spoken word.

Gesture and drawing. Piaget (in Hawkins, 1974) writes that "There is, then, no difference in kind between verbal logic and the logic inherent in the co-ordination of actions, but the logic of actions lies deeper down and is more primitive; it develops more quickly and overcomes more rapidly the difficulties it meets, and they are the same difficulties...as those that make their appearance later on the verbal plane" (p. viii).

Papert, the creator of Logo, an interactive computer program for children, describes gestures as "body knowledge" (Papert, 1980, p. viii). At about the age of two, Papert began playing with automobile parts. He loved rotating gears in circular motion against each other. Through these manipulations he acquired sensorimotor knowledge of gears: "You can *be* the gear, you can understand how it turns by projecting yourself into its place and turning with it. It is a double relationship — both abstract and sensory — that gives the gear the power to carry powerful mathematics to the mind (p. viii). Papert writes that his mathematical prowess in school and his later work in computer programming developed out of this early play with gears.

Gesture is the organic base of writing what Vygotsky called "writing" in the air. Similarly, a child's first scribbles are gestures on paper. Scribbling gradually · becomes controlled. The child experiments with figures and letter shapes, leading to the drawing of pictures. Concurrently as drawing becomes more controlled, the child names or labels her markings; she is attributing them with meaning. Conversely, as she consistently recognizes jottings and tells what they mean to her, she is "reading" them. Drawing meaningful signs is the transition to writing letters. The child develops understanding that she cannot only draw things, she can also "draw" letters.

There is a wonderful example of gesture leading to literacy in a children's story about an adventure of Frog and Toad by Arnold Lobel. One morning on rising from bed, Toad decides to list his plans for the day. He writes "A list of Things to do today," including "Wake up," "Eat Breakfast," "Get Dressed," "Go to Frog's House," "Take a Walk with Frog," etc. (p. 5). When his list is complete, Toad realizes he can cross out the first item on it. In the middle of the story copy, Lobel depicts Toad's crossing off "Wake up" with a black line drawn through those handwritten words. The young child in looking at this story is empowered by this technique. Although she may not be able to read the words, she can "read" the crossing-off line; it has meaning for her because she understands it from her sensorimotor experience.

Sociodramatic play. In Vygotsky's scheme, it is play, and specifically symbolic play, which creates the zone of proximal development for the preschool-aged child (Vygotsky, 1978): "In play a child always behaves beyond his average age, above his daily behavior. In play it is as though he were a head taller than himself. As in the focus of a magnifying glass, play contains all developmental tendencies in a condensed form and is itself a major source of development" (p. 102). Of the several forms of symbolic play, the characteristics of sociodramatic play most closely fit the descriptions of play in Vygotsky's writings.

Objects. One-year-olds typically play with toys in motion, determined largely by the nature of the object (El'Konin, 1966). Gradually, as the very young child has ample opportunity to manipulate objects in this sensorimotor way, the close connection of one specific activity with an object disintegrates. These are the antecedents of symbolic functioning; the physical attributes of objects no longer dictate how the child will use them. Instead, she begins to play with objects according to the meaning she attributes to them. This is a significant transition: from activity which is motivated by external properties of an object to use of objects in the service of play, originating from internal motivation. Vygotsky's classic example of this is the stick which becomes a horse: the child holds a stick between her legs and moves around on it in a horse-like gait.

With development, the child becomes increasingly competent in symbolic functioning. As she engages in role play, how objects are used to mean is determined by the specific role being enacted. Her use of objects evolves to an ever-broadening repertoire of original combinations and improvisation.

Role play. Part of the development of symbolic functioning is the child's desire to imitate the role of a meaningful adult. Children first play a parent; later they try the role of a less familiar but interesting person, such as a doctor, firefighter, or letter carrier. Role play develops the understanding of the concept of role (Bateson, in Schwartzman, 1978) as the following anecdote of a five-minute exchange between a child and her mother shows us:

> At the end of the preschool morning, Sarah came out to the yard. Her mother was engaged in a

conversation with a friend, which she had begun
while waiting for Sarah. The two made eye contact
in passing but neither said anything to the other.
After a few minutes Sarah went over to her mother,
and instead of the usual greeting, Sarah said:
"Mommy, you pretend you're the mommy and I'll
pretend I'm the little girl and it's the end of
preschool and we'll run and hug." Sarah backed up
to a far corner of the yard, and then ran to her
mother with her arms outstretched, yelling "Hello
Mommy!" Sarah's mother, in the spirit of the play
responded with a bear hug and the question: "Hello
Sarah, how is my little girl today?"

Role play can and does occur as a solitary form of
play, for the very young child and with the child who is
alone or prefers to be alone. But role play naturally
lends itself to social enterprise. Role playing, in
conjunction with the symbolic use of objects, develops
into sociodramatic play, where two or several children
engage in creating a drama involving socially
compatible roles (Fein, 1986). The evolution of a socio-
drama is facilitated when it is briefly postponed to
discuss role-appropriate actions, define new roles,
incorporate other children, and acquire role-necessary
props.

Coordination to rules. There is no play without rules
(Vygotsky, 1978). Children at the preschool age practice
rules, but consciousness of rules probably does not occur
until school age (Piaget, 1965). This is "the development
from games with an overt imaginary situation and
covert rules to games with overt rules and a covert
imaginary situation" (Vygotsky, 1978, p.96). In
sociodramatic play, rules of behavior are a function of
the theme of the drama. In deciding what to play,
children establish a sphere of play, a hypothetical "as
if" world that holds its own meaning for them which
Vygotsky calls the "field of meaning." The players
project themselves into the play according to the
meaning they bring to the play theme. The field of
meaning also determines how the play becomes
extended and embellished.

In play that is social, children communicate with one
another about the play. One condition necessary for

sociodramatic play is metacommunication: children discuss what they are going to say in the play scenario. A second condition is an unspoken understanding of various signals which indicate "this is play" (Bateson, in Schwartzman, 1978). These can be in the form of a glance or an action or when a child simply moves into her role and begins pretending. According to Vygotsky, play also facilitates the process of the internalization of speech, which is how thinking develops. In play, children learn to plan.

Vygotsky wrote that the preschooler's highest achievement is play. "It is here that the child learns to act in a cognitive, rather than an externally visual realm by relying on internal tendencies and motives and not on incentives supplied by external things" (p.96).

> The path from play to internal processes in school age — endophasia, association, logical memory, abstract thinking (without things, but in concepts) — is the main path of development; one who understands this connection understands the main element in the transition from preschool to school age (Vygotsky, in El'Konin, p. 230).

Development and learning. Development is an evolutionary process which is the result of the individual's inherent process of maturation and influenced by interaction with environmental factors. Contrary to widely held beliefs, development is not the sum total of one's accumulated learning experiences but rather, "each element of learning occurs as a function of total development" (Piaget, 1964, p. 38). How and what one learns is framed by her level of development. Learning is a "limited" process, limited to a single problem or situation which is stimulated by something external, such as a lesson or an experience. Learning is provoked, development is spontaneous.

Early childhood education was one of the first disciplines to approach schooling from a non-traditional perspective: that the purpose of education is to foster development (Zimilies, 1986). Programs which adhere to its philosophy attempt to achieve their goals through environments which provide nurturance, stimulation, and opportunities for exploration and self-expression. The Progressive Education movement of the 1930s in the United States espoused similar goals: in order to stimulate development, educational experiences arouse interest, enjoyment, challenge, and active thinking (Dewey, in Kohlberg, 1972).

The following quotation challenges the assumption that what children know is a direct result of teaching. Further, it challenges the traditional view of the role of the teacher. Educators must look beyond the limited lessons they teach to ways in which they can support children's development:

> We wish the child to grow up and in fact he does: we therefore attribute his growth to our own desires and our efforts (Piaget, 1930). This questionable causal attribution provides the main justification for adult efforts to educate children.
> In recent years we have become increasingly aware that adults do not teach children some of the most fundamental ideas; at best, we help provide circumstances in which children discover what they must know (Gruber, 1973, p. 74).

Conclusion

This article has used the research of Smilansky and Pellegrini and the developmental theory of Vygotsky to support the view that sociodramatic play belongs in the school environments of young children. The studies take similar positions: play facilitates children's symbolic functioning, a skill which generalizes to the more abstract level of the use symbols in reading and writing.

Systems which adhere to traditional learning theory may find it difficult to measure what is learned during play. Teachers need training to help them recognize cognitively complex sociodramatic play. Teachers also must have skills to facilitate sociodramatic play, because play that is not good often leads to disorder and does not belong in school.

Teachers who value play must make the time and the space in their classrooms for sociodramatic play. They must also be prepared to defend their positions when parents and administrators question what is learned in play. It may require a paradigm shift for many skeptics. Binger (in Emig, 1983) writes that there must be "cultural acceptance of privacy and make-believe activities as a reasonably worthwhile form of play" (p. 138).

Csikszentmihalyi (1975) states what is for me one of the most powerful reasons for children to play: ". . . a matching of personal skills against a range of physical or symbolic opportunities for actions that represent meaningful challenges to the individual" (p. 181).

REFERENCES

Cazden, C.B. (1980, October). *Children's words at Bank Street and beyond*. Paper presented at the first annual Dorothy H. Cohen Memorial Lecture, New York.

Csikszentmilhalyi, M. (1975). *Beyond boredom and anxiety*. San Francisco: Jossey-Bass.

El'Konin, D. (1966). Symbolics and its functions in the play of children. *Soviet Education, 8* (7), 35-41.

Emig, J. (1983). Non-magical thinking: Presenting writing developmentally in schools. In D. Goswami & M. Butler (Eds.), *The web of meaning: Essays on writing, teaching, learning, and thinking* (pp. 132-144). Montclair, N.J.: Boynton/Cook Publishers.

Fein, G.G. (1979). Play and the acquisition of symbols. In L. Katz (Ed.), *Current topics in early childhood education*. Norwood, N.J.: Ablex.

Fein, G.G. (1986). The social coordination of pretense in preschool children. In G. Fein & M. Rivkin (Eds.), *Reviews of Research: Vol. 4: The young child at play*. (pp. 95-111). Washington: National Association for the Education of Young Children.

Gruber, H.E. (1973). Courage and cognitive growth in children and scientists. In M. Schwebel & J. Raph (Eds.), *Piaget in the classroom* (pp. 73-105). New York: Basic Books.

Hawkins, F.P. (1969). *The logic of action*. New York: Pantheon Books.

Kohlberg, L. (1972). Development as the aim of education. *Harvard Educational Review, 42* (4), 449-496.

Lobel, A. (1973). *Frog and toad together*. New York: Harper & Row.

Papert, S. (1980). *Mindstorms*. New York: Basic Books.

Pellegrini, A.D. (1980). The relationship between kindergartners' play and achievement in prereading, language, and writing. *Psychology in the Schools, 17,* 530-535.

Piaget, J. (1932). *The moral judgment of the child*. New York: The Free Press, 1965 ed.

Piaget, J. (1964). Development and learning. In R. Ripple & V. Rockcastle (Eds.), *Piaget rediscovered*. Ithaca: Cornell University.

Schwartzman, H.B. (1978). *Transformations: The anthropology of children's play*. New York: Plenum Press.

Smilansky, S. (1968). *The effects of sociodramatic play on disadvantaged preschool children*. New York: John Wiley.

Vygotsky, L.S. (1978). *Mind in society*. Cambridge: Harvard University Press.

Zimilies, H. (1986). Rethinking the role of research: New issues and lingering doubts in an era of expanding preschool education. *Early Childhood Research Quarterly, 1* (3), 189-206.

Children As Readers and Writers in the Classroom: An Impossible Dream?

Catherine C. DuCharme

Upon entering a classroom in which children are allowed the opportunity to become readers and writers naturally, an observer may overhear children enthusiastically commenting:

"Look! I can read this all by myself!"

"I know how to spell that already!"

"Read my story."

"Do you like my poem?"

These children are becoming literate naturally in a meaningful context. For them, reading and writing are purposeful activities. Recent research and my own classroom experience confirm the importance of approaching literacy development in a language context. (1)

Characteristics of a meaningful literacy program.

As a teacher of young children, I have a deep desire to respond to what my students are trying to do as they strive to learn language. Over a period of eight years I have engaged in active exploration and experimentation to improve my own abilities to facilitate the young child's natural quest to become literate. As a result of my graduate studies and my daily classroom experience, I have observed characteristics of a meaningful literacy program for primary grade students:

1. The program is broad-based and open-ended allowing for and cultivating diversity and individual differences.

2. A multi-task approach is used for classroom management.

3. Mutual respect and trust exist between the children and their teacher.

4. Freedom, choice, and responsibility are intertwined with high expectations for student achievement and success.

5. Natural movement, interaction, and collaboration between children and the teacher are encouraged. Children teach themselves and each other. Children choose their work place and may sit in small groups with friends.

6. Children read and write for real purposes. They write letters and love notes to each other and members of the community. They write to learn and to share ideas.

7. Children are surrounded with literature. They experience the joy of listening to stories read aloud on a daily basis. They become acquainted with a variety of children's books including fairy tales, fables, poems, and comics.

8. Print is introduced naturally throughout the day as the opportunity arises. The children read announcements printed on the chalkboard. During sharing time they read clues to their peers to help them guess what they've brought to school to share.

9. The teacher continually engages in "kid-watching" — a kind of child study. The teacher keeps a file of the child's dated work to document developmental growth.

10. Children are given an opportunity to play with language. They are encouraged to invent spellings, explore phrases, and make mistakes in the process.

11. Children publish their own work. The children's stories are typed and bound to be displayed in the class library.

12. Children self-select reading material including student authored books.

13. Children are encouraged to explore the arts

through self-expression. They draw, paint, sing, dance, and pantomime.

Underlying assumptions

The underlying assumptions of a meaningful literacy program for young children are grounded in theory and research reflecting the constructivist view of language learning:

Children learn to read by reading.

Children learn to write by writing. The picture that emerges from the research in child language is one in which the language is learned naturally and gradually. (2) More than 60 years ago, Agnes deLima wrote:

> Any normal child will learn to read before he is ten, if he is exposed to books by those who value them. There is no use torturing an imaginative child of six or seven with a dull reading routine. (3)

Children learn best by themselves and each other. Piaget emphasized the importance of social interaction amongst children in the learning process. Piaget believed that "children have real understanding only of that which they invent themselves, and each time we try to teach them something too quickly, we keep them from reinventing it for themselves." (4)

Children are activity-oriented. They construct their own reality through experience. They don't necessarily develop in a logical step-by-step fashion, but rather, by interacting with their environment. Glenda Bissex refers to the Piagetian assumption that the child naturally interacts with the environment, thus reinventing his world when she writes about her son's literacy development.

> The reading materials he selected did not, like a basal series, show a neat progression in difficulty. There were plateaus, regressions, and abrupt advances in level — not surprisingly, given the several dimensions or purposes of his reading. He might on the same day attempt adult material and read an easy book. (5)

Children learn language in an integrated way.
Researchers of emergent literacy behavior agree that
the interrelatedness of reading, writing, speaking, and
listening cannot be denied. (6) Marie Clay refers to the
complex behavior of children learning language. She
writes that "a simplification achieved by dealing firstly
with letters, then with words, may be easy for teachers
to understand but children learn on all levels at once."
(7)

Young children are linguistic geniuses. They play
with language; they invent words and overgeneralize
rules. As the child learns language, he is actually
involved in creating words and generating rules. (8)
Ruth Weir's study of her son's pre-sleep monologues at
age two and a half showed that "there is linguistic
sense in the child's nonsense." (9) The data collected
showed the child's preoccupation with practicing as well
as playing with the words and sounds he uttered.
Chukovsky, the Russian poet, observed that the child
between the ages of two to five is a linguistic genius and
a natural poet. (10)

*Error plays a significant role in the developmental
process of becoming literate.* The errors children make
in their language patterns often reveal knowledge of
rules they themselves have formulated. Error can play a
highly constructive role in literacy development. "It is
now well established that the advent of error can be a
sign of progress." (11) A common sequence of events has
been observed by Donaldson and her colleagues. First
the child does something correctly. Then he starts to
make systematic mistakes. Finally he returns to his
original correct response.

Many scholars have documented the significant role
error plays in the developmental process of learning
language. Margaret Donaldson has shown examples in
oral language; she writes that children will say "foots"
instead of "feet" and "goed" instead of "went"
reflecting their growing knowledge of word endings. (12)
Kenneth Goodman has demonstrated that in oral
reading, children's errors are not accidental. (13)
Charles Read studied preschoolers and their invented
spellings for words; his findings also showed that

children's errors were systematic and often rule-revealing. (14)

Form follows function. Children want to get something done with language. As the child engages in literacy development, the emphasis for the child appears to be on getting something done with language unaffected by the correctness of form but eagerly inventing and exploring ways to work with language. (15) One child's story illustrates the point:

Figure 1

Certainly this child had a purpose for writing. He had an important message to convey to his mother. He invented spellings and played with exclamation marks regardless of correctness but rather emphasizing the content of his message.

Glimpses of classroom life

Enter into a first grade classroom that is alive where children are becoming literate in a meaningful language context. The room resembles a workshop. Many activities are occurring simultaneously. Some children are painting their word cards with water color paints. Two little girls are writing the lyrics to a favorite song together. A young boy writes about his recent trip to San Francisco.

Figure 2

I went too SanFrancisc.
It was fun.
I went too Chinutan.
I went on a chralee.
I wnt on a iverce veve krou kde roede.
It is the krou kdeist roede in the wrled.
Fhis stouree is trouy.

Another imaginative young boy writes his own fairy tale in response to a focus unit in literature on fairy tales:

Once apant a time there
where three hnters. they only
celd sheep and cows and pigs.
they celd the sheep and the
cows because you can make
heve gakits and the pig to
eat. one day they where
hnting and they saw a
manster. the manster ea eat
them aaaaaaaaam!!!!!

Once upon a time there were
three hunters. They only
killed sheep and cows and
pigs. They killed the sheep
and the cows because you can
make heavy jackets and the
pig to eat. One day they
were hunting and they saw a
monster. The monster ate
them. Aaaaaaaaaam!

In another section of the room three boys collaborate
as they draw volcanoes. One boy's story reflects his
growing scientific knowledge.

What Makes Volcanoes?

What makes volcanoes? In the middle of the earth
there is hot material. It is magma. It goes up and
makes a little crack in the earth. And it makes a
hole in the earth. It goes up and bubbles out or it
bursts out violently.

And still another little six year old girl sits alone
inventing her own word jingle:

Five litle strsts
Sat dawnd no mrs
a loy cam a moon
and sat dawnd
and say a toon
and fitint the strsts
   uwa

Five little stars
Sat down on Mars
Along came a moon
And sat down
And sang a tune
And frightened the stars
   away!

Enter into another classroom where children are
allowed the opportunity to experience the power and joy
of writing and reading. A group of kindergartners draw
and paint, reinventing their world from within. They
create images of fantasy, fear, and love. The children
dictate their stories, label their pictures, or perhaps
invent spellings of their own as they write all by
themselves. These children are on their way to
becoming literate naturally without pain, boredom, or
torture!

One five year old boy draws a ferocious dinosaur and writes:

Figure 3

THЕ DINOSAURS WAS WOKEG ₍G₎₍a₎ₗₗₙⁱᵗ

AND WAS EDE Ga.

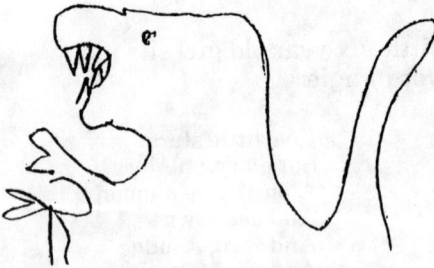

The dinosaur was walking and was eating.

A five and a half year old girl discovers that she can write and her teacher can read her words. She concentrates intently as she writes:

WON DAY it WES MY DAD BRth DAY AND We WAR
AtSIDWith BLONS AND WU LEthe BLON GO

Figure 4

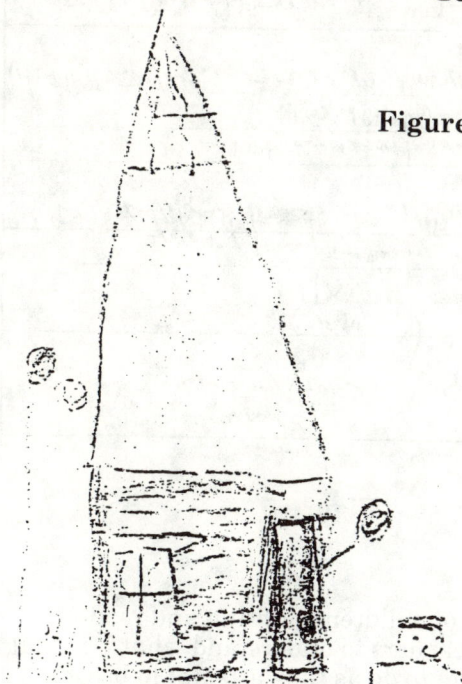

one day it was my dad's
birthday and we were
outside with balloons
and we let the balloons go.

At another table nearby a little girl five years of age plays with language. In her own words, she was "practicing cursive writing:"

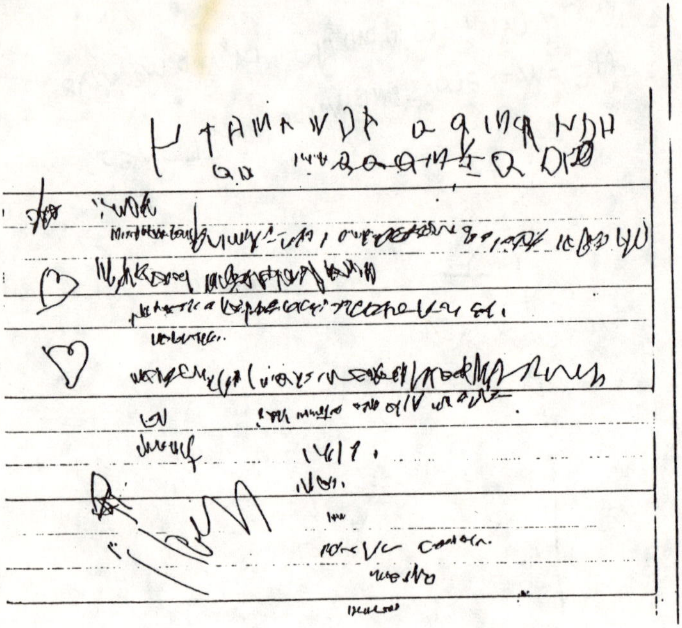

Figure 5

Careful analysis of children's writing and reading activities helps teachers to understand what it is that children are trying to do as they attempt to become literate human beings. Clearly, the example of the young girl's attempt to "practice cursive writing" reveals her knowledge of a friendly letter format.

Children want to get something done with language. Boys and girls have a lot to say and they want to communicate their ideas. In a third grade class, a young eight-year-old boy communicates reflective thought in his poem:

My Dream For the World

Figure 6

" My dream for the world (IF I had my way)

"Would make the world arise to quite a diffrent day,"

" There would not be hunger under the sun,

" And as for wars I'd proclaim there would be none,

" It would be the door to happiness my freinds,

" And as for sorrow it would be the end.

by Jeremy

It may be an impossible dream that ALL children EVERYWHERE will be allowed the opportunity to be readers and writers in the classroom. But we as sensitive, dedicated teachers can continue to lead the way so that others may follow, for it truly IS a dream worth pursuing!

REFERENCES

1 Clark, M.M. (1976). *Young fluent readers*. London: Heinemann Educational Books.

2 Shuy, R.W. (1981). A holistic view of language. *Research in the Teaching of English, 15:* 101-111.

See also:

Armantage, A.A. (1986). A comparison of the cognitive and art development of early readers of print and their yet-to-read peers: Grounds for a broad-based learning environment. In M.P.

Douglass (Ed.), *Claremont Reading Conference Fiftieth Yearbook* (pp. 281-291). Claremont, Calif.: Center for Developmental Studies.

Bissex, G.L. (1980). *GNYS AT WRK*. Cambridge, Mass.: Harvard University Press.

Huey, E.B. (1908). *The psychology and pedagogy of reading*. Cambridge, Mass.: The M.I.T. Press.

3   deLima, A. (1925). *Our enemy the child*. New York: New Republic, Inc. p. 35

4   Chomsky, C. (1974). Invented spelling in first grade. Harvard Graduate School of Education. Mimeograph: pp. 13-14. (Piaget as quoted by C. Chomsky.)

5   Bissex, op. cit. p. 141.

6   Goodman, Y. (1980). The roots of literacy. In M.P. Douglass (Ed.) *Forty-fourth Yearbook of the Claremont Reading Conference* (pp. 1-32). Claremont Graduate School: Center for Developmental Studies.

See also:

Britton, J. (1970). *Language and learning*. London: Penguin.

Clark, M.M. (1976). *Young fluent readers*. London: Heinemann.

Clay, M.M. (1975). *What did I write?* London: Heinemann.

Taylor, D. (1983). *Family literacy*. Exeter, N.H.: Heinemann.

7   Clay, M.M. (1975). *What did I write?* London: Heinemann. (p. 19.)

8   Dale, P.S. (1976). *Language development: Structure and form*. New York: Holt, Rinehart & Winston.

9   Weir, R. (1962). *Language in the crib*. The Hague: Mouton and Company. (p. 146.)

10   Chukovsky, K. (1968). *From two to five*. (M. Morton, trans.) Berkeley, Calif.: University of California Press. (Originally published in 1925.)

11   Donaldson, M. (1978). *Children's minds*. New York: Norton. (p. 111.)

12   Ibid. pp. 26-34.

13   Goodman, K.S. (1969). Analysis of oral reading miscues: Applied psycholinguistics. *Reading Research Quarterly, 5:* 9-30.

14   Read, C. (1975). *Children's categorization of speech sounds in English*. Urbana, Ill.: National Council of Teachers of English.

15   Shuy, op. cit.

See also:

Bettelheim, B. & Zelan, K. (1981). *On learning to read: The child's fascination with meaning*. New York: Vintage.

Clay, M.M. (1982). *Observing young readers*. Exeter, N.H.: Heinemann Educational Books.

Return to Reason; Individualized Reading

Jeannette Veatch

In 1960, during the Golden Anniversary Year of the National Council of Teachers of English, John De Boer, then editor of ELEMENTARY ENGLISH, wrote as follows about Individualized Reading:

> "...The doctrine that children of the same chronological age differ very widely ... is the most fully documented of all educational principles. At the same time it has been quite generally ignored in practice...
>
> But a movement based upon so sound a foundation must ultimately succeed. What form ... it will take ... we are just beginning to discover ..."

Twenty-five years later, LANGUAGE ARTS MAGAZINE, the successor to ELEMENTARY ENGLISH, honored me by asking me to write a personal memoir on the same subject. It appeared in the October 1986 issue.

Whatever form Dr. De Boer thought that individualized reading might take, it is not recognizable today in the vast majority of the nation's schools. For the truth is that there is very little evidence of such a practice in vogue. Why this is so arouses my curiosity. Perhaps it is the lack of understanding about exactly what I.R. is. Misconceptions about its character are astoundingly wrong. Thus, I have decided to try and clarify this approach which is surrounded by such monumental ignorance. Some writing labeled "individualized reading" is erroneous beyond belief.

Perhaps those struggling with what IS the dominant practice, the basal reading system might gain some insight into this alternative practice and benefit therefrom. My hope is that if teachers understand more of the how-to-do it, they might see that light around the corner. They might just move in the direction of a sensible, reasonable, instructional pattern that above all others does meet the most fully documented of all educational principles, that children of the same chronological ages differ widely.

The term itself, largely thanks to me, I guess, has become a dirty word. I am delighted with my colleague on this program who discovered the approach by way of working to make non-English speakers literate. Yet, as persuasive as his presentation is, he avoids the use of the term "Individualized Reading." "I did it on purpose," he told me. "It is too controversial." I cannot disagree.

But whatever the approach is, it is not a laissez faire practice. A specific set of procedures is essential, or the miracle of self-selection simply does not happen! It is, I suggest, a classic example of structure, but unlike mastery learning and other operant conditioning approaches, its structure is that of process and not of content. There is a huge difference between instruction that develops literacy from the inner life of the pupils in certain clear steps and stages and that instruction which follows the "Sit!" "Stay," and "Speak" of the operant conditioners more applicable to dog training than to children learning to read and write.

Perhaps you think there is nothing wrong with the way that reading is taught in America. But if there is something wrong, it can only be laid at the doorstep of the commercial, basal reading programs. There simply is nothing else being used to any degree in our schools.

Once again, I am happy to see California leading the way. The Claremont Graduate School should take some pride in the development of the current *Reading Initiative*. No matter what actual role Claremont played in this new *Open Books = Open Doors* program, it should recognize that since the late 1950s their Annual Conferences have gone in the same direction.

In another important, although little recognized study, California exposed a raw nerve. Authoritarian administrators came out very badly when reading achievement was studied in the state schools in 1980. Briefly, it was found that those schools where the teachers had the choice, and it was a real choice, of whatever reading program, and were allowed to follow it without using the manuals religiously, the achievement levels were in the upper 20 percent of all schools. On the other hand, when administrators chose the programs that teachers were to use, those schools were in the lower 20 percent. And I was told, aside from those mandated programs, one hour of paper and pencil phonics was de rigeur of each school day.

So California is again taking the lead. As Janet Kierstead asks, "Is it just another swing of the pendulum?" We don't know. But what I can do here is to describe as much as I can about just how individualized reading operates in a classroom.

Classroom management for individualized reading

Individualized reading begins with self-selection since it is essential to span these wide differences in ability. Research shows (Bortin, 1979) that children can easily and accurately choose their own reading material by the Rule Of Thumb. There must be many books to make such a choice successful. Such a supply, close at hand mind you — going to the library dampens motivation — would amount to approximately five *different* titles per child. More than that, the supply should include enough topics that no children are left wanting their hearts' desire for reading.

Next, the teacher must have prepared a class book with a separate page for each child on which pertinent data such as test results, age, and the like are written. These pages, arranged alphabetically, are for notes taken during each individual, teacher-pupil conference. Pure gold, if the truth is to be known, for report card time!

In addition, each child must have a method of keeping track of *every* book selected for the program, whether or not said book is the subject of an individual conference. (Children will confer on about two out of every 10 books they read independently. That is really enough for the teacher to give proper instruction (Veatch, 1959, 1984, 1984).) Three-by-five cards, or a section in a notebook, or some such method works well. A book report is not necessary. I view it only as a punishment for reading a book. *If* the child chooses a book that attracts him, a "report" is simply a time killer, and a chore. The child should list the author, title, and date, perhaps a descriptive phrase as "cowboy story" or "mystery." That will do it.

A crucial part of I.R. is the independent seatwork, which begins with concentrated attention on the book chosen by the Rule Of Thumb. Such reading may last 15 minutes or the whole reading period (usually about 90 minutes). Such reading must be so absorbing that an earthquake could hardly pull pupils' eyes from the page.

After reading a self-selected book, the next item on the agenda of independent work is that of writing. What is written can relate to other areas of the curriculum: letters to living people, compositions, poetry (Calkins, 1986, Burrow, 1939, 1970).

If there is time, students can work on science and/or social studies projects or do research of some type. These tasks might horrify the basal-oriented teacher as not being definitive enough. Well, if you think that these suggestions will not keep your charges quietly busy for a total reading period, blame yourself for either (1) not properly training pupils to use the R.O.T., (2) not having an adequate supply of *good* books, (3) having a weak other-than-reading curriculum, or (4) not knowing how to expect and *get* busyness.

With the class settled down as I have described, the teacher can now turn to the best of all I.R. activities, the teacher-pupil conference (Veatch, 1984). These are the best of times when you truly get to know your children personally. There are four areas for attention:

1. Questioning on why the book was chosen, i.e., the personal interest of the scholar in *that* book.

2. Comprehension of the main thrust of the book.
Does the pupil understand if it is fiction, fantasy, fact,
or what? In this sense comprehension cannot be *taught*.
It is a matter of knowing what was read. The skill of
teaching comprehension is a figment of some
professors' imaginations (Veatch, 1984).

3. Next come questions to reveal how the pupil figures
out nagging details, such as difficult words or the
meaning of copyrights, chapters, references, and the
like.

4. Last and best is the Glory Road, reading aloud so
that all want to listen and, in fact, will stop work *to*
listen. Here the teacher promptly and forcefully works
to eliminate word calling and to develop voice
modulation to differentiate between a scary story, a
funny story, or a sad story. Literary appreciation is the
heart of this aspect of the individual conference.

If the class is about 25 in number, the teacher should
be able to have a conference with about six to eight
children each day. And when teachers become proficient
in finding out what is needed to improve the reading
performance of their class, there will be time to group
those 3-5-6 children who have the *same* problem with
their reading. Maybe some kind of phonics needs
attention. Or poor oral reading habits. May it be noted
that we *never* group children on the basis of raw ability,
which, of course, is not subject to easy correction. What
can be done without teacher or pupil trauma is to
identify and teach those children with the same
anomaly in the same group and teach up a storm! It
makes Mondays so much nicer. At whatever risk, I do
think that slavish use of basal readers is the root cause
of teacher burn-out. With them pupils must be
persuaded, charmed, and/or scared into reading what is
assigned. So tragic is a classroom like that.

"Having a Go" for Literacy in a London Infant Classroom: a personal Experience

Gay C. Collins

The setting

My first encounter with a child whom I was to teach during my exchange year at Colville Primary was with Lee Sam from Ghana. "Look, Miss," his voice reverberated off the brick and glass of the empty classroom as he held aloft an orange plastic container of some sort from the local McDonald's, "How do you like my flying saucer?" Lee's commanding presence was soon joined by the others: Emmanuel, Lee's cousin also from Ghana; Simone, a local child of mixed racial parentage whose mum was expecting again; Lotus, the fair haired Italian who had spent the last year with her grandparents in Rome; Alexander, a middle class child, just up from the nursery, single parent family; Shaun, another single parent child whose father was in America and who shared the struggles of his mother to cope in the inner city; Fatima, a twin, also raised by grandparents in the Philippines, first language Tagalog, now in London to attend school; Natalie, child of longstanding neighborhood family, whose grandfather still maintained his vegetable barrow in the Portobello Market; Caroline, with an older sister already in school, working mother; Saadet, oldest child in a Turkish family; Djamel, English mother separated from his Moroccan father; Susan, whose mum just came back from a visit to relatives in Barbados; and Daniel, only child of divorced parents, mother a professional homeopathic practitioner. Not a large group at first but soon to be joined by others.

School for me and these children was an old, three-
storied Victorian brick festooned with wrought iron
drain pipes and bannisters and large windows which
looked out on a street bordered with the ubiquitous
London Plane trees, or onto the playground — a narrow
strip of asphalt bounded by high brick walls and the
backs of three-storied flats with their tiny balconies and
wash out to dry. Beyond the yard, looking down the
length of the school, through the iron gates, one could
catch a glimpse of the famous Portobello Road.
However, the sight gave few hints as to the excitement
and color of the street on Friday when the market was
in full swing or on Saturday when outsiders came to
look for a bargain and tourists came to look for
antiques.

The school was so old (over 100 years) the evidence of
segregation was still apparent in the entrances
marked BOYS and GIRLS. Mrs. Brock, a teacher's
helper, reminisced with me about attending school there
herself and learning how to wash in the outbuilding still
clearly marked LAUNDRY. I never got around to
asking her what the boys got to do.

Our classroom occupied a corner on the second floor.
It was a large rectangular space which had once been
two rooms. It had a very high ceiling but very good light
from windows on two sides. It was also beautifully
equipped to meet the needs of an infant class: the
British term for first years in school, equivalent roughly
to K-1-2. Sevens would be 'top infants," youngest go into
"reception," and in between are "middle infants" with
the provision for doll corner play, dress-up, water and
sand tables, blocks, games, manipulatives, and
listening posts. Next door was a library with many
books to which we had open access. The classroom led
directly onto the hall where we met for assemblies and
music and movement with the head or the music
teacher. Indoor P.E. on "apparatus" also took place
there. In general, it can be said that in spite of the
annoyances presented by the outmoded floor plan, the
up and down staircases, the many hidden away closets
and cupboards where one had to search for things, the
distance from the toilets for the children, the lack of

soundproofing of any kind, this school was wonderfully equipped to do the best possible job for children.

One reason for this, a wonder to me who had experienced cutbacks year after year, was that the school was in Division I, a part of the Inner London School Authority (ILEA). Directly as a result of the Plowden Report and England's massive effort at educational reform, inner city schools were considered "at risk" and so were given compensatory funding. ILEA's umbrella covers 10 divisions in London and embraces around 3,000,000 school-aged children. The Thatcher government continues to attempt to trim the fat, but the fact remains that ILEA schools generally have better educational resources in personnel programs and equipment than their fellows in the provinces. ILEA teachers also earn an extra pay allowance.

The children and I were lucky for another reason. This school boasted an exceptionally competent and caring staff. There was lots of help available in a resource teacher, an ESL teacher, a music teacher (herself a talented artist-performer), teacher's helpers, and best of all, a vivacious, forthright, and supportive head teacher who before her headship had taught for years in the school.

Getting started

So much for the setting in which these lively children and I were to create a community for learning and growing. Looking back in my diary, I wonder at my endurance. It was all so frustrating, so new, so exhausting, so scary, so exciting. There was no time to ask oneself how to begin with my disparate group — some with one year already in school, some with a term, some with only nursery experience — and all from a variety of backgrounds and cultures.

I soon realized for the non-speakers of English (Fatima and Lotus) it was to be total immersion. For all the children there was the double difficulty of getting used to American intonations, expressions, names for things. I appreciated the no-nonsense but practical approach to assimilation — "settling in," as it is called. Someone in school was found for new children to relate to in their own culture and tongue. Sibs shepherded the youngest members for as long as they were needed, staying in class with them or taking them "upstairs" while they did their work. School helpers took special interest in individual children, often because they knew them from the neighborhood. Small groups were regularly assembled to work with a resource teacher in ESL. Ethnicity was a raison d'etre of the school's outreach to the community. Assemblies usually had an ethnic theme, i.e., the celebration of the festival of Divali for the Hindu children. Songs and stories were introduced from around the world and were common currency among the children. The head considered all the culturally different children as rich resources and created opportunities for them to shine.

Right off I realized that what I had to do first while we got to know one another was to establish some routines and engage in some activities that would absorb us all. As a kindergarten teacher of some experience, I had a portmanteau from which to draw activities that I knew would succeed. We began to draw, paint, work with clay, cut and paste with the focus on finding out about ourselves; names, weighing, measuring, favorites, etc. Added were songs and stories which were enjoyed with more zest and relish, it seemed, than by my kindergarteners back home. The day itself was punctuated with many other outside activities/interruptions (collecting the dinner money, assembly, music, outdoor time, dinner, etc.). Squeezed in between were language experience activities with individuals and small groups and some simple arithmetic (maths). In the meantime, we had taken our first school journey to Richmond Park, so there were shared experiences to talk and write about. We were soon venturing out on the Portobello with one of the helpers, to the library, or to buy small purchases from the shops for the aquarium or cooking.

Gradually, as I began to find out more, I had a sense of where I could begin with a direct approach to reading instruction with a few children. Indeed, I discovered one day that Lee Sam could read beautifully already. Even though all the children showed an interest in books, some even had very special favorites they could "read" by heart and which they carried about and played teacher with. A number of them still preferred the Wendy House or Leggo to anything else.

For the sake of my own sanity and perhaps also because I didn't completely trust that each child's literacy drive could be left untended without a bit of teacher influence, I divided the class into three groups, allotting each a special time slot with me on a regular basis. With the first group, I initiated the Breakthrough Scheme, an organized language experience approach which was used throughout the school and which was accompanied by numerous sets of small paperback texts which we could read singly or together. This group was able to manage the organization of the scheme, the folders, sentence maker, etc., construct their own sentences, and write them in their newsbooks, usually accompanied by a picture. I began reading records for each, instituted a search for books that would suit them (an easy task as the school was amply supplied), and began individual interviews in which we read and talked together about the books they had chosen. These books, once completed, were sent home in a plastic envelope with a note to parents to let the child "show off" by sharing and reading their book.

The second group was not quite ready to use the Breakthrough and so I used another language experience approach, so beautifully documented by Janet Kierstead, (1) in which the child begins with his own words. These "organic vocabulary" words are collected on a ring, are pasted in the child's own book and copied, and then used in a sentence which is also cut from a strip by the child and pasted in his/her book, under the picture. Drawing is crucial at this stage as it provides the clue to meaning in case the word itself, taken out of context, is forgotten.

The third group was the smallest. With these children I took dictation to accompany their pictures and usually ended a session by reading to them. In the meantime, I took pictures of everyone, and we made *All About Me* books. To a series of basic questions regarding name, family, favorite color, food, activities, wishes, and ambitions, I typed their responses while the child supplied the picture. These pages were put together in book form and, after much handling and reading and sharing together, were sent home.

What I learned about literacy

The emerging feelings of belonging together, of being a class, allowed me to take more notice of life in the school outside of my own bailiwick. I began to pay attention to the other teachers. Often they used unfamiliar terminology to describe their programs and the children's progress. I wondered how the "shared book experience" differed from just reading to children. What were the hallmarks of a "literacy set" and how did "book knowledge" influence the "emergent reader stage?" I got some help soon, as time was devoted at staff meetings to develop a curriculum for literacy. A number of teachers were attending a course offered by ILEA's Language Center, chaired by Moira McKenzie, a well-known reading expert. Although I had felt from the beginning that the aims of education in this school were congruent with my own, I obviously had a lot more to learn. When I expressed interest, notes were collected for me from the reading course, and my head teacher gave me a book to read, *The Foundations of Literacy,* by Don Holdaway.

Holdaway defines literacy as a developmental process, of which reading and writing are merely a part. Literacy is a global term to include anything that can be said of human language; thus reading and writing are not discrete tasks but merely facets of a larger continuum embedded in language function. Literacy as a developmental process has certain characteristics which are often ignored by formal schooling, i.e., literacy learning:

is a natural process, with minimal instruction;
  is informal, in that it takes place at anytime in natural conditions;
  is self-regulating — the learner is in charge of what is to be learned;
  is non-competitive — learner's motivation is intrinsic;

is fulfilling to real life purposes and emulates the
behavior of people who model the skill in natural
use. (2)

Schools, according to Holdaway, tend to waylay this
process. "Teaching" becomes the very reason schools
fail with so many children.

> Paradoxically when the school meticulously leaves
> no stone unturned to teach literacy skills
> thoroughly, it leaves no room for children to learn
> those skills with the same efficient use of the
> faculties as they bring to bear on comparable tasks
> outside of school. (3)

Holdaway looks to early language learning to provide a
model for teaching, the assumption being that literacy
skills develop in the same natural way as spoken
language when the conditions for learning are
comparable. Every teacher of younger children knows
that some children are primed for reading tasks and
learn on their own in spite of teacher interference, while
others are unready and express this in interests that are
considered immature.

A characteristic of the self starters is that they have
acquired what is called a *literacy set* through their book
oriented home where being read to early on was
experienced as one of life's pleasures for both parent
and child. These children come to school with a deep
familiarity with a number of favorite books which they
love to read repeatedly, audience or not. They spend
more time in school with books than others and are
easily bored with the offerings unless replenished
continually. They are fascinated with print, attempt to
write freely, and will persevere, practice, and puzzle it
out confident they can unlock its meaning. They are
also more relaxed at story time as enraptured listeners.

Literacy orientation in the home doesn't wait for full-
blown language but begins while the baby is beginning
to speak. It comes out of a book environment richer than
the infants' immediate needs. The infant self-selects; his
pleas to "read it again" indicate specific tasks he's

practicing intensely in the endless repetitions and sweet familiarity of the known story. The young child also practices reading-like behavior through play and, independent of the adult, becomes "picture stimulated, page matched, story complete." (4) Rich evidence of this process is in the number of reenactments Holdaway and others have collected of children's story retellings over a period of time. Gradually, retellings of *Where the Wild Things Are* more and more come to approximate the original text. Obviously this process is not just rote learning but a deeper language processing in which children encode and express meaning at their own level of syntactic mastery.

Characteristics of the child who has accomplished a *literacy set* before formal schooling serve as a useful yardstick in assessing the others entering K-1. These children have already made an emotional commitment. They're addicted to reading, and the momentum they bring from home is very hard to squelch. Always in the minority, sad to say, they will learn with any approach. Most others will be *emergent readers*, that is they have not yet acquired all the attributes of the *literacy set* for a number of reasons.

Shared-book experience

A technique I learned to use which helped bridge the gap for those children who needed still to lay the foundations of literacy was the Shared-book Experience. Even though I had modeled the reading process when reading aloud to my class during story time or literature periods, this happy experience for me and the children could only approximate those "being-read-to experiences" at home. Even though everyone experienced those long pauses to look at the pictures, the print could not be shared. The closest we came to reading together was in our language experience stories a la Jeannette Veatch (5) when we read our class news. The shared-book experience rectifies this lack by allowing the teacher really to model what is going on when being read to. The technique is simple in presentation and also rich in possibilities for language extension. It requires large books with large texts and a book stand or easel, a pointer for the teacher, and a piece of tag for marking. Unless you are lucky enough to have a supply of large texts, the technique does require an investment of energy in the beginning, as you must make your own. Some first steps would be to find out which books the children really love to hear again and again out of a large selection of books read in the first weeks of school. Once large texts are available, all can avail themselves of the total book as the teacher points to the words, encouraging participation in unison or singly. These reading-together sessions provide wonderful opportunities for the teacher to model the strategies for decoding print as a problem-solving process, i.e.

1. noting the features in print, its orthographic elements,
2. rhyme,
3. context clues,
4. literary structure and sentence pattern,
5. phonetic principles,
6. using cloze technique (by masking certain words, children can puzzle out meaning from text).

Anything becomes grist for the large-text experience then; songs sung together, poems, recipes, how to's. Smaller versions of the shared-book texts were also available in sets. These provided a felicitous carry-over in small-group work where the children could experience "wholebookness" in the best Bill Martin sense. (6)

Other considerations

Another aspect of the classroom literacy environment was brought to my attention during a staff meeting devoted almost entirely to the book corner. The head was especially anxious to see evidence that there was ample space in each room devoted to literacy activities, not only writing surfaces with materials, books displayed attractively, listening posts, word lists, labels, but a cozy corner which would beckon to children to snuggle up with a book. I was heartened by this re-emphasis on the old notion that one's literacy surroundings serve as an essential catalyst that must be planned with care on the part of the teacher. Too often other considerations tend to take over, i.e., extra desks for the overcrowded or room for the computer console. I was glad to be reminded that the attractive book corner, at least in this school, was an expectation not to be ignored.

In the meantime, I continued to watch my emergent readers move toward a *literacy set*. Perhaps I'd previously taken all those early signs for granted. Now I learned to watch for them more carefully:

1. Directionality — moving left-right in a controlled way across the text, becoming aware of the significance of spaces and one-to-one correspondence.
2. Visual Attention to Print — beginning to learn names of letters and sound-symbol relationships, significant patterns in words.
3. Talking Like a Book — coming closer to the author's language as they reconstruct the story in their own words.

I was also learning to become a better observer, because as I felt more secure in my situation, I could let go of the reins, assured that the learners' purposes for themselves were congruent with my goals for them. The notes from the reading course provided ways to observe carefully and sensitively, i.e.:

1. Keep a diary of shared-book experiences (when used, responses, followup); shared writing experiences (why selected, teaching points, responses, knowledge demonstrated by class.)
2. Collect samples of children's unaided writing, examine and make some decisions about what they seem to know. Assess by asking, "Will you write something for me — name, ABC's, any words you know?" (Marie Clay provides an excellent resource for analyzing early writing performance.)
3. Observe how book corner is used — which books are popular, who reads alone, shares, plays teacher.
4. Examine books available for range, quality of display, variety, space, comfort for reading.
5. Observe children "at risk" by taping child reading story he knows, read to him same story two more

times during the week, retape and transcribe. Examine responses for clues to hang-ups.

There are no teacher's guides for the literacy approach except one's own good sense. Certainly working in this way requires much energy and enthusiasm. One must also be flexible to use teaching opportunities and not be afraid to let go and let things happen. Moderating control should not be confused with a laissez-faire approach, however. I like the way Holdaway puts it:

> To be tough and realistic in teaching is to put aside the temptation to control everything that children do and to accept with the respect it deserves the stumbling efforts of early performance. (7)

In my experience, English infant teachers take great interest in early struggles with print, because it is evidence of the child's uniqueness, whereas we tend to be seduced by standards of performance in our efforts to push children ahead. Our diligent efforts to move children from one basal reader to another, to get them up to grade level, etcetera, merely betrays a lack of trust in the child's implicit need to be literate. Perhaps it needs to be stated that in none of the Infant classrooms I had access to, both in my own school and outside on numerous visits, was a basal reader used. One school based its beginning reading program entirely on picture books, trade books of the highest quality. Children brought home a new book every day if so desired. The library was the focal point of the school, and parents were educated to become a part of it all. Grouping is done for the purposes of *guided reading*, not on the basis of who is in which graded text. In this situation, children are given a new text and asked to preview it first by themselves so they can build prior knowledge to bring to a discussion with the teacher. Only after much grounding in the text, interesting new features noted, opinions aired is the book read in turn or by all silently. The technique is designed not only to find out what the child knows already but is also to enhance his self respect. The end result is to teach how to preview and survey materials in order:

to locate information;

to form expectations of what stories or informational materials can offer;

to further revise, refine, and extend the understanding begun in the preview;

to sustain reading for long enough to become involved in the story;

to know about story structures and conventions (settings, events, characters, actions) which influence the expectations, understandings, and satisfactions they get from reading.

Conclusion

The culmination of my England year was the extension of a shared-book experience, *Mrs. Wishy Washy,* into a class performance for the whole school at an assembly. All the animals (the children), one by one, jumped in the "lovely mud," while Mrs. Wishy Washy (Natalie in bandana and apron) zealously tried to wash them off and Lee Sam confidently narrated. I'm grateful to have had another England year. It restored my faith in the realm of the possible and vindicated my beliefs developed from years of teaching practice. The concept of literacy as a developmental process with special dimensions that lend themselves to modeling by the teacher, in contrast to instruction by rote with inferior reading materials, has the potential of rescuing children from a terrible fate — a dislike for reading, an impoverishment of life. To all teachers of young children I would plead to try and free yourself from Ginn or whomever and all their dittoed accoutrements and, as the British would say, "have a go" for literacy!

REFERENCES

1   Janet Kierstead (1977). *Helping Children Communicate Through Written Language.*

2   Don Holdaway (1979). *The Foundations of Literacy.* Heinemann Educational Books.

3   Ibid., pp. 21-3.

4   Ibid., pp. 41-6.

5   Jeannette Veatch (1978). *Reading in the Elementary School,* second edition. New York: John Wiley.

6   Bill Martin. *Teacher's Guide: Instant Readers.* California State Series.

7   Holdaway, op. cit., p. 105.

Where Do the Words Come From?

Elizabeth Jones

Children's growth in literacy is a process of increasing familiarity with the written word. In our schools, where do the words come from?

Most of them come from controlled-vocabulary lists, selected by some logical adult as the words easiest to learn. Reading and writing are taught as logical-sequential exercises in which words are constructed out of sounds and proceed sensibly from simple to complex. There is a new letter sound every day, reinforced by worksheets. There are basal readers. Reading is seen as learning to decode, and handwriting and spelling are systematically taught out of context.

I have taught both preschool and primary, as well as teaching teachers, and my background is human development. And so I'm continually distressed by the way in which our schools ignore developmental theory — all the things we know about the ways in which children construct knowledge and in which each stage of knowing builds on the one before. Piaget, who offers the most comprehensive theory of cognitive development, has helpfully defined three kinds of knowing: (a) physical knowledge, what I know about the world from acting on it with my body; (b) social knowledge, what I know about the world because you told me; and (c) logical knowledge, what I know about the world from thinking about my experience and ordering it in order to construct meaning. (1)

Mostly, in schools, literacy is taught as social knowledge. Some things *are* social knowledge, including the names of things in any language. We learn them by being told that 'b' says 'buh,' that this is a room and

those are chairs and my name is Betty. But competence
in literacy goes far beyond rote knowledge, as anyone
knows who has listened to a child trying to read
phonetically — buh, ah, luh — with no sense of context
or story. Written language is a complex structure which
must be rediscovered — constructed — by each reader
and writer. The construction of knowledge takes place
in a context of personal meaning. The words I learn to
read, the words I write, need to mean something to me,
to connect with my experience.

Human beings are meaning-makers. Viktor Frankl,
who spent World War II in Nazi concentration camps,
has written that we cannot survive without meaning. (2)
Both to know and to take effective action, we need to
know *why*. Children learn to talk through engagement
in meaningful interactions. Literacy is effectively
learned in the same way.

Children construct language

Children learn through play, that is, self-initiated
activity which grows out of their curiosity about their
environment. The higher carnivores are curious, and the
omnivorous primates are especially curious. They spend
a lot of time hypothesis-testing: If I do this, what will
happen? If there are words in the environment, children
will be curious about words.

> Children learn to talk in an environment full of
> talk. They learn to write in an environment full of
> writing and writings. (3)

> Certainly children are predisposed to learning oral
> language. But it is misleading to claim that being
> surrounded by talk is enough. It is *being included
> in talk, and being treated like a competent
> language partner* that makes the difference. (4)

> Children learn language from people who respond
> to their meanings before their forms. (3)

Oral, written, and read language develops along a
continuum, and gesture and drawing are integral stages
in the process. Writing precedes or at least parallels
reading, because children are *active* learners.

> Language grows from being telegraphic and
> context-embedded toward being elaborated and
> explicit. (3)

Children construct language for themselves by a
process of successive approximations. The toddler who
begins by demanding "Ball!" will move to "Gimme ball"
and, eventually, to "I want the ball." It is a self-
correcting process. Children's errors are logical, like "I
runned" and "I goed." They show us the child's
thinking.

Adults can support this process, or ignore it, or
interfere with it. Any parent will spontaneously make
the effort to learn her toddler's language: "Bubba."
"Yes, here's your bottle." Nor do most adults correct
children's drawings. But few adults seem to make the
effort to read children's approximations at writing;
rather, they show children how to do it the adult's way
and thus interfere with the child's own process.
Schickedanz observes:

> . . . the external circumstances that appear to
> support natural oral language learning have often
> gone unrecognized. Similarly, the natural
> beginnings of literacy development have been
> overlooked or dismissed as unrelated to the
> conventional reading and writing behavior that
> appears later. As a result, we seem to have
> overestimated the extent to which oral language
> learning is natural (i.e., the result of simple
> unfolding no matter what the social
> circumstances), while we have underestimated the
> extent to which written language learning may
> occur in the absence of direct instruction. (4)

Constance Kamii has written about Piaget's view of
autonomy as the aim of education. Autonomy implies
the capacity for independent action and for critical
thinking, both moral and intellectual. Critical thinking
is learned by practice in the face of disequilibrium.
Disequilibrium is faced most productively in the
company of one's peers, because they aren't authorities
and are thus fair game to argue with. Opportunities for
children to work together and question each other's
work teach autonomy; correction by the teacher teaches

heteronomy, dependence on others. (5) If we correct the child's writing, he becomes dependent on us for the right answers. "Teacher, how do you spell. . . ?" is the incessant cry in primary classrooms, and no amount of word listing and dictionary making eliminates it as long as it is clear that correct spelling is the standard. If this standard is applied from the beginning of the writing process (rather than at the end, where it belongs), it inhibits risk-taking in vocabulary choice. Teaching primary children, I got thoroughly fed up with journal writing which was limited to "I played. I played with Josh. We had fun." Lyon, who was cautious, wrote that every day, while Maya, who had no fears about invented spelling, wrote pages and pages.

Are we willing to learn children's language, even as we are helping them learn ours? Watzlawick, a psychotherapist, has described the difference between those classic therapies which require the client to learn the therapist's language in order to analyze her problem (and which may take months or years to complete) and those brief therapies in which the therapist works to understand the language of the client, to put himself in the client's place and understand his perception of the world.

> It should be immediately clear that this approach
> requires a change in a therapist's own stance.
> Instead of seeing himself as a firm rock in a sea of
> trouble, he becomes a chameleon.

At this point many therapists prefer to dig in, but

> . . . for others, the necessity of ever new adaptations
> to the world images of their clients is a fascinating
> task. (6)

Most teachers are accustomed to being a "firm rock in a sea of trouble." If we spell correctly at school, that keeps the teacher, who knows how to spell, in charge. If we permit children to construct their own spelling, using the logic of phonics as they understand it, the teacher is no longer in sole charge; she may not be able to read it. By rote, the 6-year-old can learn to use adult spelling, but that short-circuits the natural process of invention and leaves children unsure of their own powers. To support the child's process, teachers can use all available cues to understand children's writing, just as they are using all available cues to try to understand ours.

> Typical phonics instruction and teacher behavior during such instruction often attempt the impossible — getting children to hear what the teachers know.

The children who do understand what teachers say are those

> who come to school already knowing what the teachers mean. (4)

To avoid this impasse, it is possible to change the rules of teaching. Paley, who used to give children the answers, changed her approach when she started listening to children: "I now wanted to hear the answers I could not myself invent." (7) Thus teaching becomes dialogue rather than telling, and the words come from the children, not just from the teacher and the textbooks.

Paulo Freire, teaching illiterate adults in Brazil, based his work on the same sort of dialogue. It is up to the teacher to find out what words have meaning in learners' lives, to bridge the gap of understanding between teacher and learner. Words have power. The words that people can learn best are their own words. People, adults or children, who find their own voice can change their lives. (8) Working with Maori children in New Zealand, Sylvia Ashton-Warner discovered the same thing. Key words are a base for dialogue: Tell me your word. I'll write it down. Children, she emphasizes, are creatures of passion; and words, written or spoken, are an art medium through which feelings can be powerfully conveyed. (9)

Thornley quotes a 4-year-old child's response to a visitor who was showing some art works to a group of children: "And what kind of art do you like to do?" Diana responded cheerfully, "Writing!" (10)

Learning in a context of meaning

An English study of the conversations between 4-year-old girls, their mothers, and their nursery school teachers found that both middle-class and working-class children displayed more language competence in adult-child conversations at home than at school. Home conversations were about topics of mutual interest to adult and child: shopping, meals, vacations, and the past, present, and future doings of family members. Mothers gave information as much as they asked questions. In contrast, teachers typically asked questions about play and toys in the here-and-now, and their questions were often ineffective in connecting with children's interests and stimulating genuine conversation. They were behaving like good preschool teachers, but it was mothers who, because of their shared interests with their daughters, were providing more effective language experience. This was especially true in working class homes. Even though working class mothers used somewhat less complex language at home than middle class mothers, their daughters' language was higher in both quality and quantity at home than it was at nursery school. (11)

Home conversations are embedded in the context of personal meaning. School, Donaldson has pointed out in *Children's Minds,* is different; it is preparation for life in a society which places the highest value on thinking abstracted from personal meaning. This is the kind of thinking required by science and mathematics and engineering and the management of bureaucracies — *disembedded* thinking. In Donaldson's words, "The better you are at tackling problems without having to be sustained by human sense the more likely you are to succeed in our educational system." (12)

How can we make the necessary bridge from embedded to disembedded thinking, especially for those children whose home experiences are different from those at school, who do not "come to school already knowing what the teachers mean?" (4) It is no accident that it is working class children who most often fail to become effectively literate in our schools. When my daughter went to kindergarten, her teacher said approvingly to me, "Nancy knows so much." But even as I basked in her praise of my first-born, I was aware that Nancy didn't know more than the other children in her class, some of whom knew two languages, and some of whom were highly responsible in caring for younger siblings. What mattered was that what Nancy knew was *what the teacher knew*. To *be like the teacher* is to be valued, in all those schools which value not diversity but conformity.

To build bridges, we need to begin by connecting with children's own divergent meanings, not plunge them into formal systems like phonics. From a developmental perspective, literacy is acquired because it is *meaningful*. Meaning is personal and idiosyncratic, so each child's "key words" (9) will be different: Who are the people in my life? What do I love? What do I fear? What do I do? Words, like all symbol systems, give power to name one's own experience and provide catharsis through the expression of feelings. Stories told by others can connect with and objectify our own experience.

Meaning is also interpersonal: How can I communicate with others? Functional literacy includes the ability to use signs and messages, to read in order to find out and to write in order to give important information.

Meaning is also inherent in playfulness; we play for pleasure. Words can be played with, apart from their meaning. What strategies can teachers use to build bridges? How can classrooms serve as places where meaning is acknowledged, created, and extended?

Bridge-building strategies

Where do the words come from in a typical kindergarten or primary classroom? How many of those words would children also hear and see at home? Certainly this depends on the literacy of the home and on its style. Some families post calendars, have books, write notes on the refrigerator door. Probably more families read newspapers than books. But do you ever see newspapers in kindergarten, except under the easels?

All children draw at home, if they have tools to draw
with. Young children invent writing, too, distinguishing
it from drawing by the direction of the strokes or the
shape of the forms. Where print is available to observe
and adults to answer questions, children copy letters
and use sound cues to invent spelling — beginning with
the first letter, then adding the last, and eventually
getting around to the vowels in the middle. *Come* may
begin as C, then CM, and progress to CUM or CAM or
COM. MSTR is surely recognizable as *monster*.

Many parents show children how to write their
names, and children like to practice. Harste (13) tells
about posting a sign-in sheet in a nursery school; and
Janie, who teaches a Spanish-speaking kindergarten,
liked that idea. Each day she posts two long strips of
paper on the cupboard doors, telling the children,
"When you get to school, write your name here." If a
child says, "I can't," he isn't given a model (though he
can find his name elsewhere in the room), he's simply
asked to try. Any and all marks are acceptable. They
may vary from an unrecognizable scribble for Jorge, a
wobbly M for Marco, to a carefully lettered
ESPERANZA stretching the width of the page and on
to the next line for the ZA.

It's daily practice in literacy, with successive
approximations to be celebrated, not corrected. (14)
Janie saves the sign-ins as a record of children's
growth. This is practice in context; it makes sense. You
don't sign in at home, but at home your mama knows
you're there. When we come to school we sign in. There
are lots of kids at school. Your teacher needs to know
you're here.

Standing in line is what people do when they need to
take turns. You do it at the store, or at Disneyland, It's
fun. You can talk to your friends, and you can watch
how they write. (15)

In Anne's kindergarten next door, several children
initiated an activity during choice time, collecting words
from around the room and copying them on little slates.

"Teacher, what does this say?"

"Show me where you got it.
What do you think it says?"

"Paper towels. . ."

Not a standard word list, but real words in the
environment. All young children learn to read words in
environmental context: STOP, Corn Chex, McDonald's.
They don't just use the code, they use the context as
well. That's embedded thinking. These weren't key
words in terms of being the children's own, but they got
to discover them, to exercise curiosity, to practice
copying, and to talk about them with their teacher and
each other. It's one of the possible ways of making *word
collections*. And children learn about divergent thinking
if the word turns out to be not *paper towels* but *Standard*.
Different words can belong to the same thing. (16)

Schools are forever teaching convergent thinking:
there is only one right answer. That's not good practice
for living in a changing world, full of diversity and
many answers. Children who have already learned the
teacher's answer at home will get it; those who haven't
probably won't.

Right answers are typically reinforced with
worksheets. A child might get a worksheet that expects
her to draw a line connecting each picture in the right-
hand column to one in the left-hand column. Maybe the
right-hand column has pictures of hats, and the left-
hand column has pictures of the people who might wear
them. The right answers have been decided by the
person who drew the worksheet. They may be confusing
to children who haven't experienced the stereotypes
conveyed in the pictures, and they don't draw on all the
different things children have learned through their
own diverse experiences. I don't know why that
worksheet was about hats, but suppose, for some reason,
hats are what you want to teach about. How could you
do it divergently?

One way is to provide *talkalot kits*. (17) You bring in
the most varied collection you can find — of hats, or
brushes, or shoes, or buttons, or food containers. And
you make it available to play with, if you're working

with young children; physical knowledge comes first.
After a while, you talk about it. You might ask, "Why do
people wear hats?" Sometimes teachers who ask
questions like this have a particular answer in mind
and are fishing for it. Given a different answer, they
say, "Yes, but that's not what I was thinking of." Here,
though, all answers are right. The task is not "Guess
what I'm thinking" but brainstorming: let's see how
long a list we can get.

Another question: "What are all the things you can
think of that people put on their heads?" All answers
are right. Our word collection will reflect the diversity of
our experience.

What can you do with a word collection? You can put
it up on the wall. Some young children enjoy choosing
words to copy. Some might use the words in their
journal writings. We might do a group story. It's the
process that is important, taking off from any topic.
Everything in the world is potential curriculum for
children. We're celebrating diversity, not everyone all
alike.

In many classrooms children's work looks all alike.
That's not they; it's their teacher or the book she got her
ideas from. It doesn't make connections for children,
and it leads to invidious comparisons. "I like how neatly
Sally is writing," says the teacher, holding up Sally's
paper for all her uncoordinated peers to see. That's all
there is to respond to when everyone is doing the same
thing: neatness, speed, correctness. And so some
children will be consistently less successful, and they're
usually the children whose home experience is most
different from that of the school. But if everyone is
writing, drawing, or painting their own experience, then
the teacher can respond to *content* — to children's
divergent thinking, to the interesting differences among
them.

Another way to organize a word collection is to web it.
In the nicest parent conference approach I've ever seen,
the teacher begins by calling each child to her, writing
the child's name in the middle of a large paper, and
then asking, "What words go with Joanne?" When

Joanne and her teacher finish talking, her paper might look like this:

Figure 1

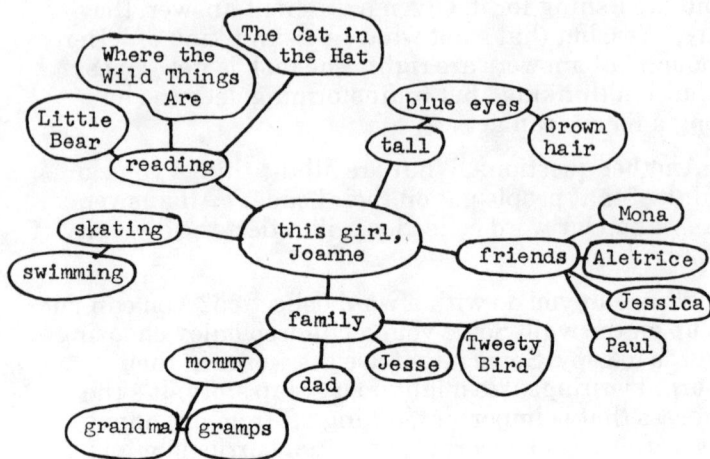

It's a key-word process elicited by a direct question, "Who are you?" It's shared with parents when they come for their conference: "These are the things Joanne said about herself. What would you say about her?" (18)

Alice wrote her own name in the middle of the chalkboard and asked her third graders, "What are all the words you can think of to describe me? Polite words, please," she added as her two troublemakers began to snicker, She webbed it as they went along, something like this:

Figure 2

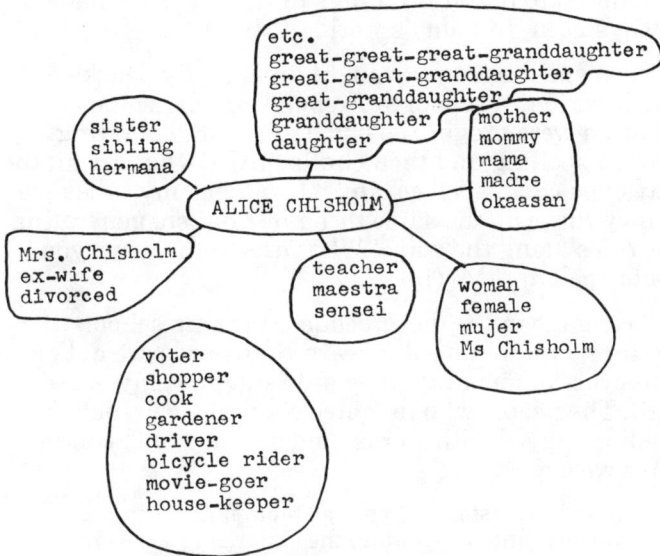

The words weren't all synonyms; they reflected Alice's several roles in several different languages spoken by children in her class. She used her judgment about categorizing the words, negotiating with the children to encourage divergent thinking. *Daughter* was her own contribution, queried by one of the less mature children who asked, wonderingly, "How can you be a daughter if you're a mother?" Alice promised to bring in a picture of herself as a baby, with her mother, and told all the children that their homework was to ask their mothers whose daughters *they* were.

How can you have different words for the same thing? That's confusing, and enriching. Differences are important to think about. How can different people do things differently from the way we do them at our house? How come my daddy lives with my mommy and yours doesn't? How come you talk Spanish and I talk English? How come you hit me when my daddy told me never to hit? How can we deal with our differences? By *thinking* about them, with adult help in a divergent mode, in order to promote autonomy — the making of independent moral and intellectual judgments. (5) In a traditional, homogeneous society convergent thinking is functional to maintain things in the way they have always been. In today's world, it isn't.

Even spelling can be taught divergently. Duckworth has described a school in French Canada where children were taught the basic rules for generating French spelling and then challenged, "What are all the ways you could spell *cousin*?" I watched my colleague Nancy Place do the same thing in English, generating the rules along the way: "What are all the ways you could spell *night?*" (19)

To engage in the disembedded thinking school requires, children need to learn that words are not only conveyors of meaning, they are things to play games with. The people who invented English or French spelling played with words, and so can we. The more ways we get, the better.

> Note that instead of feeling stupid for creating an
> unconventional spelling, the children feel clever.
> And they know that whoever may be dumb, in
> making spelling such an arbitrary exercise, it's not
> they! (20)

Another way to play with word collections is structural analysis. Some teachers in Albuquerque (21) invite children to analyze the *morning message*, written on the chalkboard: Take a piece of colored chalk and choose something to circle all the examples of — all the words that begin with m, perhaps, or all the upper case letters, or all the lower case t's, or all the periods. Choosing enables each child to find a challenge he can meet; a child who doesn't yet read can competently circle all the o's. All choices are valid and interesting to the other children, who are looking for the patterns too. It's non-competitive, but when the chooser says she's finished, other children can say if they see any she has missed and add them if she can't find them.

Message analysis is a way to help children learn the formal aspects of language while taking their diversity into account and validating individual choices. Everyone can do it, and their differences are what keep the process interesting.

Children learn through play — through making choices in a rich environment. Children are fascinated by words. If the classroom environment is full of words and the tools for writing and displaying words, children will copy others' words and invent their own. (22) There needs to be time for uninterrupted writing/drawing on topics of the child's own choosing, and time for conversation, for stories, and for classroom events worth using words about. (23) When the same writing topics and skills tasks are assigned to everyone, both initiative and competence decrease, and the writing which teachers have to read becomes less interesting.

Historical perspective

If we know all this, why don't most schools teach literacy this way? Change is slow. Kamii, analyzing the history of theory and practice in psychology and education, says that in any science the first theories are based on common sense knowledge of how things work. The next theories are associationist, positing simple linear relationships; in psychology, behaviorism is such a theory. The next theories are interactionist, positing circular, complex relationships; in psychology, Piaget offers such a theory.

People stick to simpler theories as long as they can. The heliocentric theory was resisted for centuries, because the geocentric theory was more in tune with common sense. (24)

In education, common sense tells us that if we tell children something, they will learn it. Behaviorism reinforces common sense, telling us that if we tell children something and reinforce their correct response, they will learn it. Like any intermediate theory, this is partly true, but there is a lot it doesn't explain. Interactionism tells us that telling is effective only for social knowledge; logical knowledge is constructed by each individual, classifying her own experience. What teacher would use a theory like that if he could get a simpler one to work?

For many of the children in our schools, the application of simpler theories is not working. Children do not all learn literacy in the same orderly way; the construction of knowledge is an unpredictable, messy process, very annoying for teachers who are in need of order and a right way to do it. Teaching in an interactionist mode is active, and it requires divergent thinking on the part of teachers: How can I surround the children with print? How can I connect with the words that have personal meaning for them? How can I integrate writing, reading, and the arts to help each child find her own voice and thus build literacy on understanding?

REFERENCES

1   Labinowicz, ed. *The Piaget Primer*. Menlo Park, Calif. Addison-Wesley, 1980, pages 44-45.

2   Frankl, Viktor, *Man's Search for Meaning*. Boston: Beacon Press, 1959.

3   Bisssex, Glenda, *GYNs AT WRK: A Child Learns to Write and Read*. Cambridge, Mass.: Harvard University Press, 1980, pages 786-791.

4   Schickedanz, Judith A., *More than the ABC's: The Early Stages of Reading and Writing*. Washington, D.C.: National Association for the Education of Young Children, 1986, pages 8 and 19.

5   Kamii, Constance, "Autonomy as the Aim of Education: Implications of Piaget's Theory, "in *Number in Preschool and Kindergarten*, Washington, D.C.: National Association for the Education of Young Children, 1982.

6   Watzlawick, Paul, *The Language of Change: Elements of Therapeutic Communication*. New York: Basic Books, 1978, pages 140-141.

7   Paley, Vivian, "On Listening to What the Children Say,"*Harvard Educational Review 56:2*, May 1986, pages 122-131.

8   Freire, Paulo, *Pedagogy of the Oppressed*. New York: Seabury, 1970.

9   Ashton-Warner, Sylvia, *Teacher*. New York: Bantam, 1964.

10   Thornley, Katherine Bakst, *The Writing Table: The Young Child as the Emergent Reader-Writer*. Pasadena, Calif.: Pacific Oaks College, unpublished master's project, 1987.

11   Tizard, Barbara and Hughes, Martin, *Young Children Learning: Talking and Thinking at Home and at School*. London: Fontana, 1984.

12   Donaldson, Margaret, *Children's Minds*. Glasgow: Fontana/Collins, 1978.

13   Harste, Jerome C., Woodward, V.A. and Burke, C.L., *Language Stories and Literacy Lessons*. Portsmouth, N.H.: Heinemann, 1984.

14 Rich, Sharon J., "Restoring Power to Teachers: The Impact of 'Whole Language,' " *Language Arts 62:7,* November 1985, pages 717-723.

15 Jane Meade-Roberts, San Vicente School, Soledad, Calif., personal observation.

16 Anne Solomon, San Vicente School, Soledad, Calif., personal observation.

17 ESEA Title III, *Prolexia,* Riverside County Schools, Riverside, Calif., n.d.

18 Sharon Wagner, Puget Sound Primary School, Seattle, Wash., personal observation.

19 Nancy Place, Pacific Oaks Children's School, Pasadena, Calif., personal observation.

20 Duckworth, Eleanor, "Language and Thought," in M. Schwebel and J. Raph, eds., *Piaget in the Classroom,* New York: Basic Books, 1973.

21 Albuquerque Public Schools, *Elementary Language Arts Program for Classroom Teachers,* 1983. 725 University, S.E., P.O. Box 25704, Albuquerque, N.M. 87125.

22 Loughlin, Catherine E. and Suina, Joseph H., *The Learning Environment: an Instructional Strategy.* New York: Teachers College, 1982.

23 Graves, Donald H., *Writing: Teachers and Children at Work.* Portsmouth, N.H.: Heinemann, 1983.

24 Kamii, Constance, "Leading Primary Education toward Excellence," keynote address, California Association for the Education of Young Children, San Diego, March 9, 1985.

The Third Person

Robert Muffoletto

Often the designers and producers of audio, written, and visual messages hold misconceptions about the interpretative strategies utilized by their audience, the receivers of their message. Simply expressed, it would be to "get their message across to their viewer, listener, or reader." My purpose today is to explore that activity so that we as producers of messages may better understand how it is that we make meaningful messages — and how it is that others may or may not understand them.

When we watch a television program, read a book, talk on the telephone, look at an advertisement in a magazine, or speak face to face with another individual, we are taking part in some form of communication. Messages are being created by some producer, transmitted through some medium, and received through a single sense or multiple combination of senses by some receiver. How these messages take on meaning for both the producers and receivers is complex in nature. It is not, as our "common sense" would at times like to tell us, a simple process of speaking or photographing or, simply listening or looking. To speak and to listen involve a complex process of designing and producing meaning, so that it makes sense to both the speaker and the listener.

For example, in preparing this presentation I had to consider not only what I knew, what I wanted to say, how and when I was going to say it, but why I wanted to say it. I had to consider not only the ideas I wanted to express, but the forms my ideas would need to take in order to make sense, not only to me, but to those I assumed would be experiencing them at this conference. As I was constructing this presentation, I had to

210

consider both you and myself as receivers or readers of
my text. Through alternating breaths, I was both a
producer and reader of my own text. Throughout this
critical and reflective process, I was in continual
conflict: Would my audience know what I meant?; Did I
say what I mean, and did I mean what I said?

To understand the process by which we make and
understand messages, it may be useful to view this
communication process in three parts. First, there are
producers of texts. Second, there is the text, or the effect
produced by the producers. And last, the reader or
receiver of what is produced. By text, I am referring to
something that is read by a reader or receiver. Texts
take on many different forms. For example, there are
social texts and there are visual texts. When a person
enters a social space, they tend to explore the
environment, look for recognizable patterns, make
associations, and compare these to their expectations
and history. Through the process of reading the text, the
meaning of that space is formed by the reader (Fish,
1980). This creation of meaning happens when you
enter a meeting room, walk down the street, or go to a
dance. The same happens when an individual
experiences a film, a television program, or an
advertisement. By reading the provided text, an effect is
produced which leads the reader/receiver to make sense
or meaning from what is being experienced (Muffoletto,
1986).

As I will discuss later, the producers of a text, be it an
individual or a team process, draw upon their
expectations and projections for the design of their
message. In producing a message, the producer will
draw from a number of meaning domains organizing
the material available to them, creating the message or
effect they wish to create. The intent of the producer,
then, is to produce or construct messages or effects. The
reader of the message or text will experience the
material created by the producer, reading it for
meaning. What is important to consider here is that the
reader of texts, the messages producers create, must
first recognize that there is a text to be read. To
understand a metaphor, the reader of the text must first
understand that what they are reading is a metaphor.

Semiotics

Semiotics as a model for studying communication is an investigation into the meaning of signs and symbols, how they work, how they are used, and what they mean (Culler, 1981). To help us understand this process of communication, message design, and the transmission and consumption of ideas, the field of semiotics offers to us a useful model. (In referring to the act of communication, I include the domains of verbal and non-verbal expression. In this sense, communication includes both written and verbal language as well as the non-verbal languages of gesture, clothing, posture, hairstyle, and social and physical context.) Semiotics, also termed semiology, was introduced in 1906 by the Swiss linguist Ferdinand de Saussure. It is based upon the notion that in language and in its generation of meaning, there must be an underlying system of conventions and distinctions which make this meaning possible. To better understand the process of communication and the generation of meaning, we need to look into the semiotic model.

Today I am concerned with two general areas of semiotics. First, the relationship between a sign and its meaning. And second, the way signs are combined into codes. Simply put, a sign is material that represents or stands in place of something else. A sign represents an object or concept. For example, when we read the word, "box," the marks on the paper are not the box we refer to. When I make the sound, "box," the sound has no natural connection between itself and the object in front of us called a box. In both cases, the marks on the paper and the sound created refer to an object that may or may not be present. By itself, a red light has no meaning, but when associated with the concept of stop, the red light appears to have a meaning. What produces the appearance of the red light having meaning is not the red light as a material object, but its relationship to a concept and the social acceptance of that association as being meaningful. Thus we think "red" means stop. A sign is something that stands in place of something else.

In semiotics, these two conditions, the material object

and the concept, are termed the signifier and signified. The signifier is material that is placed in association with a concept (Figure 1). The concept is called the signified. This association is called the sign. A sign, then, is the association formed between a signifier and a signified. A sign is the result of the association between material and a concept. Meaning is the result of this association.

Figure 1

Meaning is formed between the association of a concept or signified and material or signifier.

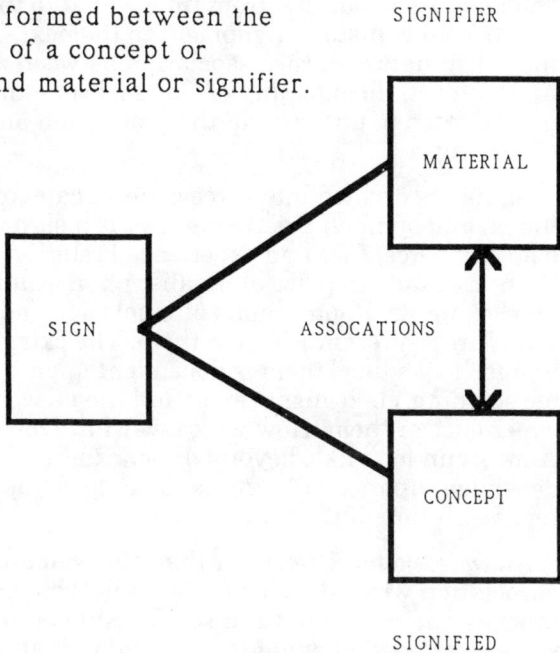

SIGNIFIER

MATERIAL

SIGN

ASSOCATIONS

CONCEPT

SIGNIFIED

    A sign then becomes meaningful through an association which is socially and historically defined. Because the association formed between the signifier and the signified is arbitrary, it is subject to change over time. History, then, determines how a sign is read; i.e., what a sign means. In other words, a sign is part of an historical process. The signifier, or material, may remain the same, but the signified will change. An example of this historical process is found in the use of the index and middle finger extended over the head forming a "V" shape. During the early 1940s in England this gesture was associated with the concept of victory. During the late 1960s in the United States this same gesture was associated with peace. The same gesture when located in a third-grade classroom may be a response to a math question or a request to leave the room. In all cases, the material or gesture did not change, but the concept did. Other examples include the changing meaning of words or the meaning of sounds. In both instances the meaning of each may vary greatly from culture to culture, from time period to time period, and from one historical moment to the next. The historical nature of the association between material and concept, the meaning of things, is one that must be investigated to understand the production and reception of messages.

Signs are divided into three general categories: icon, index, and symbol. Briefly, an *icon* is a sign that holds a strong perceptual and experienced relationship to the thing it stands in place of. Realist photographs offer a good example. Photographs of Uncle Joe and Aunt Lynn are re-presentations of them. The extent that the image "looks like" them is dependent upon the medium of recording, its transmission, and the viewer's experience of them. How we know what Uncle Joe and Aunt Lynn look like, beyond direct experience, is dependent upon a willingness to accept something as a representation of them.

An *index* is more abstract than the icon and its association with what it stands for is arbitrary. With indexes, there is no natural relationship between the representation and what it represents. Examples of indexes include written and spoken language and a range of gestures. An index points to or refers to something, and its association to that something is arbitrary. The resulting meaning of signs that refer to or point to something is a social construction. It is a meaning that has developed over time.

The third category, the *symbol*, may combine both the icon and the index. Its meaning is broader in scope and usually conceptual in nature. Again, the image of Uncle Joe is an icon, but it may very well enter the symbolic domain when viewed from certain perspective. Uncle Joe's image may stand for all the uncles of the world, or "uncleness." The meaning of a symbol comes from how a culture utilizes it and not what it depicts or refers to. Symbols deal more with how we may think about something. Symbols are instruments of thought (Langer, 1942).

Countless examples of icons, indexes, and symbols could be noted, for our world takes its significance from them. We begin to give meaning to what is around us because of the concepts we associate with the material world of our existence. All too often we forget that the meaning that is assigned to representations is arbitrary and exists only because we say it does. In other words, we have learned to see the world not as it is, but as we or others have made it.

Codes

Our second interest in semiotics is the organization of signs into a system of meaning. This system is referred to as a code. The meaning of a code, like a sign, is not naturally formed. A code, like a sign, is socially and historically determined. It is the socially agreed upon meaning of signs and the organization of signs into socially meaningful codes that make communication possible. Found in our different cultures and social communities are many different and some similar coding systems. These include the written, spoken, and visual languages. There are systems of meanings or codes which form our understanding of rituals, art, clothing, and morals. In essence, "to be socialized and be given a culture [is] to be taught a number of codes, most of which are quite specific to a person's social class, geographical location, [and] ethnic group..." (Berger, 1982, p. 34). It is important that we consider the notion of codes as an organization of signs, because it is through the process of codification that messages are created. It is the placement, the juxtaposition of visual events within an image, that affects the reader of the image.

As I have mentioned, codes are systems of organization. As an organization of signs, codes may be read from two different perspectives, from the syntagmatic, and the paradigmatic (Figure 2). *Syntagmatic* refers to the linear organization of signs, their syntax. It is through the juxtaposition of signs, where they are placed in relationship to each other, that a building of meaning occurs. *Paradigmatic* refers to

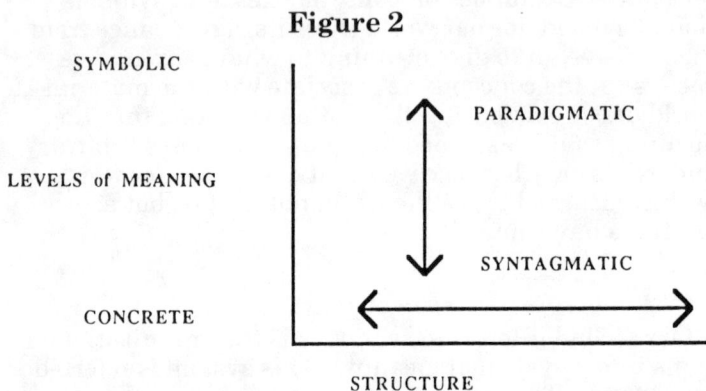

Figure 2

SYMBOLIC

PARADIGMATIC

LEVELS of MEANING

SYNTAGMATIC

CONCRETE

STRUCTURE

various levels of meaning that may be assigned to a sign. It is because of the paradigmatic meanings of signs that multiple interpretations may occur. In our concern for how messages are created and read, the syntagmatic and paradigmatic elements are critical to consider. How producers, designers, and writers organize and present their text, their images, will have an effect on not only how the reader reads it, but what the reader will read.

The message or meaning of the constructed text, be it a television ad or program, a magazine story or advertisement, a billboard sign, or actions of a dancer on the dance floor, is the result of the syntagmatic organization and paradigmatic reading of the signs utilized. Returning to my earlier discussion of signs, the meaning of a dance, a television ad, or a handshake is arbitrary. By themselves movements, pictures, and handshakes have no meaning. It is only through their association with concepts that they become meaningful for both the producer and reader of the text.

Producers, texts, readers

Producers. It is only through the indepth analysis of the productive process of authors and their resulting texts that the nature of the text can be revealed. The text, through a deconstructive method of analysis moves away from being an object void of human concern to one that is the result of social, political, and economic forces. The text, as message, is no longer understood to be a window to the world but as a mirror of those forces that produced it.

In creating messages, visual or otherwise, producers organize signs and utilize various codes to create their meaning. The codes selected work with various devices through which meaning is created. For example, photographers have at hand such devices as tone, color, lighting, size, lens depiction, and other formal and surface qualities. In selecting these various devices, they correlate them with what may be called props. Props include actors, clothing, background and foreground environments, and gestures. Once selected, the devices and props are arranged within the limitations of the frame in such a manner as to provide an intended effect or message. Other devices available to producers of messages are sound, the sequencing or editing of effects, and the selection of a delivery or transmission system. Each of these basic devices, when combined with other devices within a code, work toward the expression of some intent or message.

Earlier, I mentioned that signs are arranged in systems or codes in order to take on meaning. What this means is that when a sign is placed within a certain system, and these are social systems, it acquires a defined context or framework to become meaningful. For example, we may consider the various codes of labor, family, government, health, religion, happiness, futures, authority, and success. A producer then may draw from a number of different coding systems to create its message (Figure 3). Consider for a moment that signs, when placed within a system of thought, constitute the understanding of family. At first, you may have various men, women, and children. Through some gesture or unifying element they are doing

Creating the Text from Existing Codes
Figure 3

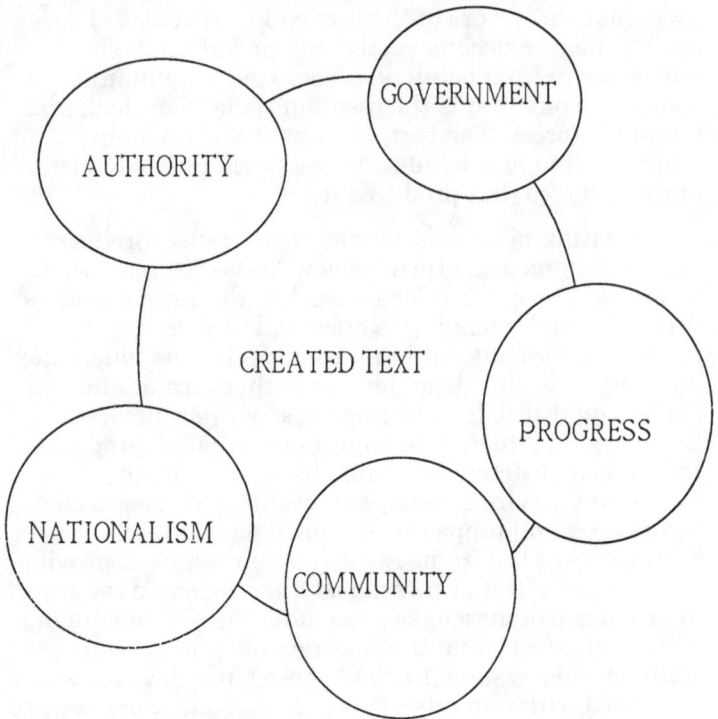

something in common or together; they are associated with the notion of family. In a 1950s photographic exhibition at the Museum of Modern Art in New York City, Edward Steichen, then curator of photography, constructed a landmark exhibition entitled "The Family of Man." In forming this exhibition, Steichen incorporated from the existing code of family a statement that re-confirmed the notion of family. In other words, he utilized an existing code, one which his audience could understand and relate to, and then reproduced and maintained the meaning of that code through his exhibition. In the process of selecting and organizing an intended message, Steichen, as a producer, drew upon a number of other factors which, when in concert with other elements of the code, determined what the effect or text would be (which may be different from its received meaning by different audiences). As suggested above, these other factors included a history of working with images and a history of reading other messages.

It is important to note that in order for a producer to create a message, the producer must first know what a message is and how it may be depicted in order to create one. It is the same as needing to understand what a "pun" is and is not in order to make them. Also, the producer of any text must have something to say, an intention, i.e., the message. And very importantly, he must consciously or unconsciously know how to say it. These few criteria may appear to be simple and direct at first glance, but to consider their implications in the production of messages is a complex and involving critical process. To deconstruct the productive process through which producers and authors create messages is to consider the basic assumptions by which meaning is created. In doing so the investigator will unveil a range of meanings and various interpretations, never quite arriving at or answering the question, "What is the meaning of this text?" In the final form, the producer has produced an effect that first of all means something. The sense that "it" works, "it" says something, suggests that the message is there. The text has been written.

What we now have before us is the text, something to be read or experienced by a reader. There are a number of issues that need to be considered in the analysis of the created textual effect. In doing so we cannot put aside the awareness that the text was created by someone or a number of people, all of whom have invested interest in the production of messages and their effects on the receivers of those messages.

The Text.

The text as an effect does not exist in isolation. There is a universe of constructed texts through which the reader comes to know and relate to the text they are experiencing. Texts also exist within a history of other texts. In a cross-textual historical analysis, it will assume a position with other texts. Actually, some may consider that the text really never exists at all, that is, until the reader of the texts says it does (Fish, 1980). To consider the historical or cross-textual relationships between texts, one must be a reader of the text, and identify whatever "that is" as a text to be read. For after all, a text is something we produce and read. By its very existence it implies a reader and a producer. Without either the text would not exist.

Once a text or texts have been identified for analysis, we can better come to know the forces that create texts by looking at their treatment of specific issues. For example, to better understand how the text creates consumers, we have to explore the notion of consumerism across many texts: What are the images? What are the audio treatments? What is being said by both? How often do the messages appear? When do they appear? and Who is watching them when they do appear? These are only a few of the considerations a researcher may consider in a cross-textual analysis of messages about one issue, consumerism. To better understand the broader implications of social messages, we must look across the channels and back in time. We do this because it is the collective message that has impact and effect on the consciousness of the individual. It is through the consumption of many texts, of many messages, that a consciousness or vision about "what is" is formed. Those who control the production and dissemination of messages, over time, have a major effect on the horizons of those who read those messages.

Readers: The Third Person.

In reading any message, visual or otherwise, we are in fact becoming the third person in the process of communication. By actively pursuing the text, we have no choice except to read the text. By doing so we become the third element, or third person in this process. The first element or person is the producer or author of the text who constructs his or her message through the encoding process. The second is the text or produced effect, understood as part of a larger collection of texts; the third, the reader or receiver of the produced effect.

In considering the meaning of texts, readers cannot be viewed in any meaningful manner as being mere receivers or receptacles of messages. The receivers of text cannot be seen as passive within any communication mode, for the reader of any message is not passive; in fact, the reader of any text is very involved in a range of perceptual and cognitive activities which determines the meaning of the text for that individual. For example, upon viewing an image of a visual text, the reader must take part in a number of activities. First, the information must pass through the perceptual process, one which leaves the three dimensional world of spaces and objects to one of chemicals and electricity. Second, he or she must recognize that there is something there to be read, that in fact there is a text. Third, the reader must recode this information and make sense out of it. The recoding process involves many activities, one of which is prior experience, or a history with similar texts and similar codes. At this point one of two events may occur: the reader will recreate the intended meaning of the producers or the reader will create a new, unintended meaning. The first is a matter of reproduction, the second of creation. In either case, meaning is localized somewhere in that space between the reader and the text. Meaning from a reader's perspective is something created by the reader in the process of responding to the created effect: the reader creates his or her own text, his or her own meaning. The concern here is not for the analysis of the production and dissemination process, but for the reception of the effect and its response. From this position, the text is not something concrete that can be defined, it is something that must be experienced.

For each different reader of a text, there will be a different interpretation. Affecting each reader's reading of a text will be his or her personal history and experience with other texts, agreements and their conflicts with the message read, and personal ideologies. Because of a reader's history with other texts, the meaning of any text changes. By returning to re-read a text, a different text is experienced because of the reader's prior experience of that text and other texts. After all, it is only because of a reader's history of reading texts that he or she recognizes that there is a text to be read. It is only through experiencing what a photograph or film *is* that we come to understand our relationship to it. For example, without the prior experience of looking and thinking about what art is, its history, and its conflicts, the reader of a modernist painting may not see it as art or as anything at all. The response may be that they do not know what it is. But from their perspective they do know what it is not. It is not art.

We have almost arrived at the point of considering where the meaning of any text exists, but there is one more consideration we must briefly explore. Stanley Fish (1980) refers to the notion of interpretative communities and their effect on individuals in the reading process. Fish suggests that individuals are members of various formal and informal social communities, and as a member of that community shares with other members philosophical and ideological horizons. While being a member of one interpretative community, an individual, at any time, may be a member of other supporting or conflicting communities. These communities may or may not be as formally structured as a political party or as informal as all the uncles of the world. For example, one may hold membership in the interpretative community of parents while also holding membership in other interpretative communities: laborers, gender, racial, ethnic, national, cultural.

Because of one's placement within various communities, the reader of any text may read that text differently at different times. At one time an individual may read the text as a parent, as a party member, or as a member of a specific gender group. In any case, the reading of a text is dependent upon the reader's position at any specific time. As a member of an interpretive community, the individual shares various viewpoints, beliefs, values, and horizons with the other members of that community. Because of that commonality of experience and expectation, different readers' responses to various texts will be similar to others who share similar experiences and expectations (Culler, 1981). It is through this notion of interpretative communities that we can begin to explain the similarity of responses or readings given to a specific text. It is important to note at this point that different interpretative communities would interpret the same text as a different text because of the historical, social, and political position held in relationship to that text. The produced effect, the image, does not change, just the reading of it.

REFERENCES

Berger, A. *Media Analysis Techniques*. Beverly Hills: Sage Publications, 1982.

Culler, J. *The Pursuit of Signs: Semiotics, Literature, Deconstruction*. Ithaca: Cornell University Press, 1981.

Fish, S. *Is There a Text in This Class*. Cambridge: Harvard University Press, 1980.

Holub, R. *Reception Theory: A critical introduction*. New York: Methuen, 1984.

Langer, S. *A Philosophy in a New Key: A study in the Symbolism of Reason, Rite, and Art*. Cambridge: Harvard University Press, 1942.

Muffoletto, R. "Reading the Visual Text: Dancing to the Music." In R. Braden (Ed.), *18th Conference on Visual Literacy*. Commerce, Tex.: International Visual Literacy Association. In press.

Tubes 'R' Us

Edward Moreno

For most outsiders, Southern California is the land of
the sun and the flowers, when the rest of America
freezes. Or our crazy freeways. Sometimes, the Missions.
Invariably, Disneyland...and, "The Meskins."

For me, as a public broadcaster it's an area of service
which includes: 11 of the most populous counties in the
nation; over 300 identifiable communities — some 100 of
them in Los Angeles County alone; the top financial
center of the United States and its prime shipping and
export center. Southern California is the heart of the
magic Pacific Rim, a combined economy of over $170
billion, which makes our area the twelfth most powerful
economy in the world.

The area is 35,000 miles square; and, it is inhabited by
more than 13,000,000 people living in about 5,000,000
households, nearly all of them equipped with, at least,
one television set. These households, for our purpose,
are termed: "TV homes." Who lives in them?

> Six percent of the people are of Asian descent: the
> largest concentration of Koreans outside of Korea;
> the fastest growing settlement of Chinese in the
> United States; the largest nucleus of Japanese and
> Japanese-Americans; and, more Samoans than in
> all of Samoa.

One percent of the population are of Native-American
descent. We have the largest Amerindian population of
anywhere in the United States, too. We also have a
healthy share of blacks, about 15 percent of all our
people. We have the largest concentration of Filipinos
outside of Manila. And, nuclei of varying sizes of Arabs
— the real and the make-believe; Canadians, Germans,

Indians, Pakistanis, Polish, Ukrainians, Russians, Armenians, Iranians, Irish, English, and, of course, Hispanics.

In an oblong lined by Alvarado and Highland, Pico and Sunset Boulevards, you will find: Argentinians, Bolivians, Cubans, Puerto Ricans, and other Caribbeans; Chileans, Central Americans, and people from everywhere in Latin America, including, of course, the Mexicans, who have been here the longest.

As an ethnicity, Hispanics represent 40 percent of the total non-black population, plus 2 percent of the black population in Southern California, although the 1980 census statistics do not seem to show that reality. Since 1970, Hispanics have provided over 70 percent of the area's net natural growth — the balance between births and deaths.

A 1970 population map published by Los Angeles County showed the white population as the dominant statistical factor. In the 1980 version of the same map, while still dominant, the white population factor was down to only 52 percent; blacks were also down a fraction of a percent, while Asians and Hispanics were up, to a combined factor of 35 percent.

The Southern California Association of Governments, "SCAG," census data resource for our area, now projects a total of 16,000,000 area residents by the year 2,000, with the index of white population down to 42 percent and the combined minority factor up to 58 percent.

For marketers, these population changes are an absolute delight, because Southern California sits right at the center of the "magic Pacific Rim," where half the world's population, mostly "minorities," also live.

Closer at home, the Los Angeles Unified School District predicts a total of over 700,000 pupils, by 1997, of which only 12 percent will be white. And this, according to the alarmists, will require that we declare Anglo children a "protected" group.

Others, the realists, feel that what mandated integration failed to accomplish, that is, balanced statistics, will be attained by human nature and unrestricted mating among ethnic groups; and that, at some time in the near future, school statisticians will be able to live comfortably, forever after, with the phenomenal population of multi-ethnic numbers, which when translated give us the largest group of the most beautiful children in the entire world.

There is more. Despite Hayakawa and the rest of the purists, that new mass may end up chattering in a brand new language, which for lack of a better term could be called: "Asi-bla-rab-Chicanglish," or Californian, for short.

Unbelievable? When Morrie Greenberg was principal of King Junior High, one of the schools in the central area of Los Angeles, I asked him to list the languages which richly spiced his daily life at the school. He listed 32 varieties. Belmont High School, not far from King, can list three times as many.

The President, the Governor, Congress all insist we must train these kids for competitiveness, because unless we do it well, not just our entire economy, but even our retirement plans will be sunk. How are we preparing our future multi-lingual merchant-dukes of the Pacific Rim?

In congested schools and overcrowded classrooms; with periods of 30 weeks of 30 hours, minus luncheons, recesses, and holidays; and, by professionals of whom we are so afraid that we restrain them with "teacher safe curricula," and pay them less than we pay our garbage truck drivers, while tooting our own horns about our high regard for and lavishness towards quality education. Then, we wonder why, despite such "high regard" and "lavishness" towards them, the schools still produce a growing mass of intellectually spastic predators for whom society is an easy mark, and school graduation is anathema.

Of course, there is an alternative educational system. It is known as "media;" and, Southern California is the "media capital of the world," with 80 radio stations, 25 television stations, 150 cablecasters, some with 100 active channels; and, VCR's, disk, teletext, instructional television networks, and all kinds of programs from The

Beggar's Opera to Zanytoons. In this alternative, the same kid who retches after 20 minutes in the classroom seat, with others around, petrifies by himself for seven hours, day by day, year after year, before the "boob-tube."

The finances of this alternative system are formidable. In Los Angeles, broadcasting and cable alone gross about $2 billion a year. Nationally, the figures are even better. The "kidvid" market alone is over $200 billion strong. It teaches the kids, in 15-second commercials, to accept anything from cereal boxtops, to useless or dangerous toys, which besides the 15-second commercial messages, become 30- or 60-minute-long sales pitches. It also teaches them to read ancillary materials, called "comic books," and reinforces the curricula by leading them to buy, borrow, or steal audio and video cassettes.

Unlike its school counterpart, this system is not afraid of teaching manners and morals, including piggishness, covetousness, violence, greed, and the cultural refinements of callousness, cruelty, murder, and promiscuity. With all of that, and our societal contributions to family erosion, the "double-income-no-kids," and to economic splits, what chance does traditional education stand?

The projections for the future are even darker. One reads in the March/April 1986 issue of "The Futurist" the following sobering thought: "The age of schooling is over. A new post industrial learning enterprise is about to replace the outworn infrastructure of industrial age education."

Perhaps, we shouldn't be ready to roll up and play dead. Something very interesting is already happening, and this should give us new hopes. In the fall of 1986, cartoon ratings dropped 39 percent in viewership, and, that trend seems to continue, while at the same time, the number of viewers for both public television and its cable imitators, is on the continuous increase, particularly among younger audiences. We can accelerate the return of youth to true education by learning from, or even by joining the competition, and mastering its techniques and tricks.

Instructional Television, Television Advisory Councils, and even Community College Consortia aren't the sole answer. In fact, they may also be part of the problem by being designed as "teacher safe" materials, too. The modern teacher has to learn, not only to transcend the limitations of the curriculum, but to plot and even connive.

Take "Language Arts," for example. The assigned text materials aren't the only form of language. Dance, graphics, photography, and other visual means are now incorporated in the efforts to help youth learn in the new environment of visual literacy. Both kids and adults are hungry for sense-making information that may help them meet their own needs. "Nova," "National Geographic," and "Nature" specials may help in the areas of natural or social sciences; but, even cartoons can help us teach human values or socialization.

To insure the desired effects, teachers cannot rely solely on program descriptions; they must be totally familiar with the programs they want to assign and then be ready to discuss what the students have seen. They must be ready to help youth understand and transact the contradictory or difficult issues presented by any viewing assignment. Often prohibitions against prolonged television watching bring only rebelliousness and disobedience. Interaction with parents and caretakers may help them learn when to say "yes," and how to substitute passive watching with active creativity.

Several schools in Southern California are already experimenting with visual literacy programs. Among them, the programs at Rowland and San Pedro High Schools, are excellent models that use a multi-disciplinary approach to what was formerly considered simply an entertainment form. Some of these programs, and their products, are helping children free themselves from the rigors of learning language in the abstract, and are teaching them how to attain eurythmia between image and word.

As consumers, teachers and administrators must learn to demand better products from instructional television suppliers. The bases for their demands are the needs of the ultimate consumers, the children.

Cable companies are well known for their desire to provide "cable drops," that is, installation to schools for free, or at reduced rates. Interactive cable offers two-way communication which will provide many new opportunities to creative educators for use of the media, both for classroom or home work. "Homework Hotline," a very inexpensive program shown daily during the school year by public television KLCS Channel 58, in Los Angeles, is a favorite of school children, not only among pupils of public schools, but among students of parochial schools in the area. Its popularity is judged by the more than 80,000 calls received by the station during the 36 months the "show" has been on the air. Another great help for teachers of social studies is the increasing number of cassettes of programs with English subtitles coming from abroad or from local non-English-speaking broadcasters. Their use provides better understanding of the foreign cultures and forces students to use their reading skills.

The local public television stations bring to students alternatives in viewing. But even with them, no broadcaster worth its pictures remains a broadcaster for long unless the programs it produces are watched extensively. Media watch groups can bring about media change. As proven by the ratings game, in any media empire, the true emperor is the public, who can make or break any program, either the simplest and modest format or the most lavish and well-heeled show. It is up to us to learn how to use the resources of media to help develop the kind of leadership and world awareness needed to make Southern California the real gem of the Pacific Rim. Whether in front of it as users, inside of it as topics, or behind it as manipulators, the tubes are us.

To better understand the effects of modern media on all of us, and the better use of them, I have prepared a very short list of some books and articles that I have found of great value:

Comstock, George, Steven Chaffee, Natan Katzman, Maxwell McCombs, and Donald Roberts *Television and Human Behavior*. New York: Columbia University Press, 1978.

Mander, Jerry *Four Arguments for the Elimination of Television*. New York: William Morrow & Co., 1978.

Moody, Kate *Growing Up on Television*. New York: Times Books, 1980.

Winnick, Marian Pezzella, and Charles Winnick *The Television Experience: What Children See*. Beverly Hills, Calif.: Sage Publications, 1979.

Notes on Contributors

PAUL AMMON is an Associate Professor of Education and Director of the Developmental Teacher Education Program, and MARY SUE AMMON is a Research Psychologist at the University of California, Berkeley. Developmental psychologists, both have long-standing interests in cognitive development and in language and literacy. Besides working together on the "Learning English through Bilingual Instruction" project, they are co-directors of a research project on science writing and learning at the Center for the Study of Writing at Berkeley.

JOAN BLUMENSTEIN is the Senior Librarian for Children's Services at the Orange Public Library. She has served on the award committees for the Southern California Council on Literature for Children and Young People and the Friends of the U.C. Irvine Library. She is currently Vice President/President Elect of the Children's Services Chapter of the California Library Association.

RAYMOND BURIEL, Associate Professor of Psychology and Chicano Studies at Pomona College, serves as Chairman of the Intercollegiate Department of Chicano Studies of the Claremont Colleges. His research interests in generational differences in personality development, sociocultural adjustment, and education issues pertaining to the Mexican American have resulted in numerous publications.

GAY COLEMAN COLLINS retired from the Claremont (California) School District after 25 years teaching children in kindergarten through the sixth grade. During that time she spent two years teaching in England as a Fulbright Exchange Teacher. She is currently teaching on a part-time basis in Carpinteria and Santa Barbara, California.

DANA DAVIDSON is an Assistant Professor of Human Resources at the University of Hawaii, teaching courses on infant and child development focusing on the role of time, place, culture, and events in the determination of healthy growth and development. Her research emphasizes the changing family and expectations for children. JOSEPH TOBIN is an Assistant Professor of Human Resources at the same university. He is the author of books and articles on Japanese culture. Summers he conducts tours to Japan for educators through the University of Maryland. DAVID WU is a Research Associate for the Institute of Culture and Communication at the East-West Center in Honolulu. His research interests include ethnic identity, national policies on minority groups and cultural issues of East and Southeast Asia. The author of numerous articles on these subjects, he is currently conducting a "Cultural Studies Feasibility Project" at the Center.

CATHERINE C. DuCHARME teaches in the Teacher Education Internship Program at The Claremont Graduate School where she is a doctoral candidate. Her interests include emergent literacy behavior, early childhood education, and the history of education, specifically, curriculum history.

DOLORES A. ESCOBAR is Associate Dean of the School of Education and a Professor of Elementary Education at California State University, Northridge. She is the author of *The Challenge of Teaching Mexican-American Children, Social Studies Instruction at the University Elementary School,* and articles on language development and language acquisition. A former director of the Title VII Bilingual Teacher Training Project at Northridge, she maintains a strong interest in multicultural education and educational equity.

JUAN M. FLORES is an Assistant Professor of Elementary Education at California State University, Northridge, where his teaching emphasizes the language arts. A former elementary and secondary school teacher, he has published articles dealing with the education of Chicano children and youth.

CHARLOTTE S. HUCK is a Professor Emeritus from The Ohio State University. She is widely known for her book, *Children's Literature in the Elementary School.* Miss Huck is a past president of the National Council of Teachers of English. She is the recipient of The Ohio State University Distinguished Teaching Award and the Landau Award for Distinguished Services in Teaching Children's Literature.

ELIZABETH JONES is a member of the Faculty in Human Development at Pacific Oaks College in Pasadena, California. Her publications include *Teaching Adults: An Active Learning Approach, Dimensions of Teaching-Learning Environments,* and *Joys and Risks in Teaching Young Children.*

JANET KIERSTEAD is a private consultant in educational research and in curriculum development for such clients as the California State Department of Education and individual districts and counties. Kierstead holds the Ph.D. in Education from The Claremont Graduate School where she is a lecturer in the Administrative Credential Program.

STEPHEN D. KRASHEN is a Professor of Linguistics at the University of Southern California, Los Angeles. His publications range from linguistics through the neurophysiology of language and language learning, to school applications of research and theory in language development. A prolific contributor to the literature on language development and second language learning, he is also in demand as a lecturer in these fields.

STEPHEN B. KUCER, Assistant Professor at the University of Southern California and program director for the graduate reading and writing specialization, has published several articles on reading and curriculum integration. He received the Ph.D. from Indiana University with a major in reading education.

EDWARD MORENO is Vice President of Community Services for television station KCET, the highly regarded Los Angeles member of the nation's public television network.

ROBERT MUFFOLETTO is Assistant Professor in the Teacher Preparation Center of California State Polytechnic University, Pomona. He coordinates the Educational Technology and Media Studies Graduate Program at Cal Poly and serves as President of the International Visual Literacy Association. He has published in the area of media studies and education.

ROBERT L. OSGOOD is a doctoral candidate in education at The Claremont Graduate School. He holds the M.Ed. degree from the University of Vermont. His doctoral dissertation will be a history of the development of special education in the Boston Public Schools.

ABBIE SHUFORD PRENTICE received her Ph.D. degree from The Claremont Graduate School and is currently a speech pathologist with the Burbank Unified School District, Burbank, California. Her research interests include children's literature, reading development, and verbal/non-verbal communication.

GRETCHEN REYNOLDS is a Master Teacher and Visiting Faculty Member at Pacific Oaks College. A former teacher and Staff Associate in The Claremont Graduate School Teacher Education Program, she is a doctoral candidate in Education at The Claremont Graduate School. She received her M.S. in Education from the Bank Street College of Education.

JEANNETTE VEATCH is a Professor Emeritus from Arizona State University. Nationally known for her writing and lecturing about non-commercial approaches to the teaching of literacy, she is the author of several texts and many articles. Her current project is the development of a series of video-cassette recordings illustrating a naturalistic approach to the teaching of reading and writing. She is heading a non-profit organization which is developing and distributing them.